Cannabis Farms

A NEW CROP

BASED ON CHARACTERS CREATED BY

LLOYD SHELLENBERGER

AND

SCOTT KINDRED

By SCOTT KINDRED

Dedication

For the Mijo family

John

Donna

Johnny

Tina

Cary

Acknowledgment

Lloyd and I would like to thank the following people whose encouragement is greatly appreciated.

Ariel Armstrong

Donnell Owens a.k.a. Quentin Terrentee-nose

Marcella Florez

Melody Florez

Casey Shellenberger

Randall Frakes

Contents

Foreword

By Randall Frakes

I have had the pleasure of mentoring our author Scott Kindred for a few years now. Scott has come a long way from his high school newspaper and Hollywood spec script writing days. He and his creative partner Lloyd Shellenberger have come up with very funny characters from the greatest generation to the most recent one. Plus a very formidable villain in the Abyss Corporation.

Some of my credentials are writing the novelization of the Terminator movie, being a contributing author of James Cameron's Story of Science Fiction, and the writer of the feature film Hell Comes to Frogtown, among others. Most of my writing efforts are in the science fiction genre, so I must ask the question...

What is comedy?

To you, it could be something completely different than it is to me. At the end of this book, however, we will both know we read something very funny. We, the readers, will find out how an average American farming family, the Monticetos, overcome their hardship and strive against the odds to follow the American dream and pursue happiness. I would describe the story like the grapes of wrath of comedy, each family member travels their own humorous route. The story sprouts in 2016, just before the voter initiative, Proposition 64, legalized the adult use of cannabis in California.

Now sit back, strike up some herbal refreshment if you are so inclined, and enjoy reading how an average American family takes on an evil corporation. Thank you for reading. Say, this book would also make a great movie. I love to laugh. Signing off, this is Randall Frakes giving 'Cannabis Farms A New Crop' two big thumbs up!

Chapter 1

The small town of Hephzibah, California, was known in its early years for being a cradle of infrastructure, incorporating one of the first farms of its kind to grow out of northern California's Napa Valley. It was expected that, in 160 years' time, starting in the 1860s when the land first broke, there would be vast fields of fresh grapes and greenery throughout the land, all sprouted from the earnest effort of the dedicated farmers.

Through the ages, these farmers toiled and broke both dirt and spines to till the land, mix the fertilizer and harvest the freshest wheat and corn which the land could provide. Wait. Wheat and corn? Some farmers just made the wrong choice of what to grow.

Presently, the last cereal crop farm standing is the Monticeto farmstead. It's hurting. All that hard work and effort crapped out sometime in the 60s and never recovered. The new deal of decades past and the failure of the United States farm bill ensured that soil degradation became too expensive to overcome. Year after year, smaller crop yields were inevitable.

The man at the head of the family, Jimmy Monticeto, would discover a new crop, one which was easy to grow, but as legislation and drug administration rulings came into power across the country became impossible to sell until now. And that brings us to today. Hephzibah, California, is a small slice of slowly moving Americana frightfully adjacent to the ever-encroaching presence of a gentrifying city force that still thinks building towns in the desert is a cool thing to do. Global warming takes its toll as the land is blasted by the sun and scorned by the rain.

The people are an eclectic mix of the city faithless who moved out in droves but still wanted to stay close enough for an afternoon drive to get some street tacos on the weekends.

It's a town with pride flags and Confederate lingo, where people get in fights over what regional dialect of Spanish they speak, where there's no job earning more than $50,000 a year, and where sometimes traffic gets stalled by either a burned-out bulb in a traffic light or by the slow crawl of a tractor hogging up the whole damn street. Like today.

Old people tend to drive slowly. They take their time and smell the roses, so there's no rush. Tractors also are slow. Grandpa Elbert, at the over-ripe age of 100, combined both forces of nature to cause a blockage in the roads.

The town only had one good main road, and he was keen to take his time down it. Anyone with complaints could Dear John his John Deere to the license plate, an old rusted flake of metal that read KEISTER.

The traffic got so bad that Jimmy had to get out of his Ford Explorer to see what was going on, braving the heat of the NoCal desert away from his precious air-conditioned cabin. There were plenty more cars between him and the main obstacle, namely a smoke-spitting pickup that spat a gray stain on the hood of Ford's white hood. The streets were aroused with a cacophony of honking.

He walked over to the sidewalk and saw the backup was so bad a few box trucks were parked on someone's sparse lawn. They had a weird logo, a hollow circle with a sort of ring that spiraled unevenly from the top into the side, and wide-spaced sci-fi font that read ABYSS CORPORATION.

They looked like movers, taking stuff from a little farmhouse while the family cried tears of…heatstroke. Not despair, probably. Then Jimmy saw the foreclosure sign and chose to look away.

Up ahead on the sidewalk was an uptight, cocksure, proud man, middle-aged but younger than Jimmy and with more but whiter hair. He watched the scene with glee, surprisingly. Until a sharp, airy whistle caught everyone's attention. Straight from the tractor as it blocked off the fancy, sleek Jaguar that the businessman parked in the grass.

"Try foreclosing' on this, you bastards!"

It was Grandpa Elbert, feet on the seat, ass in the air and overalls around his thighs. The businessman, and the whole line of cars, in view of the elevated perch, got a full view of an early moon.

Jimmy shook his head. He recognized that ass. And more so, that voice.

"What are you playin' at, you crazy old coot?" he said to himself.

The taunting display seemed to stir up more than just honking. Jimmy ducked his way into his car. That was Elbert, better known as Grandpa and actually Jimmy's father-in-law. He had to hide, or someone might recognize their relation by the shape of his tuchus.

Chapter 2

Jimmy made it home miraculously. Contraflow traffic stopped long enough for the rest of the traffic to use the opposite lane to pass Grandpa while he continued his slow crawl through town. The box cars remained behind. They'd have their own hard time moving out, to no one's shock.

But things were better back home, at the Monticeto farmhouse. Jimmy walked in and hung up his hat on the antler of a wall-mounted jackalope and his jacket on the horn from a bison which was marked by a plaque underneath reading BUTT SCRATCHER.

The smell of dinner guided him to the dining room, where two seats of six were already occupied. His wife, Madeline, a thin and well-aged woman with curlers locked in her hair, met him with a hug and a goose. He returned the favor. Their nine-year-old daughter Brandy shook her head disapprovingly at the middle-aged love affair.

"I love your tater tots!" Jimmy exclaimed.

Brandy sighed disgustedly. "You two need a new code word. Can't you wait until you're done eating, at least?"

Jimmy rolled his eyes, gave her a kiss on the forehead as he passed, and took his seat to a mostly fried dinner spread. The only thing unfried were the bills, which had been stacked up for so long that they became an impromptu tablecloth to catch the grease from the edges of the plates.

"The horizontal bop," Brandy chastised," knocking boots, the nasty - I'm not a little girl anymore."

"Where did you learn all this stuff?" Jimmy asked.

"Sex ed, Dad, OMG, Duh! I can't wait to have a boyfriend."

"You're grounded for life," he said. "No boyfriends."

Madeline spoke up. "Go wake up Grandpa and call him down for supper."

Jimmy knew that wouldn't work. The old coot wouldn't be back until tomorrow morning. Not because the tractor was slow. He'd just get lost once he got blackout drunk and wind up in the desert at midnight again.

"Y'know what?" Jimmy interrupted. "Let him sleep. He can have an extra Ensure when he gets up."

She shrugged. "He'll only cuss us out, I guess." She set down a casserole straight out of the oven. It was still bubbling. It wasn't cheese or a gratin or anything like that. It used to be solid, but the devilry that went on in her kitchen somehow liquefied the contents into a swampy, steaming mixture. Jimmy and Brandy shared a look of abject horror.

"Looks good," he said with grit teeth. "What is it? Should it be doing that?"

A huge bubble formed up with a sort of sigh and popped. Jimmy stretched his arm to cover Brandy as she gasped.

"Dad, don't piss it off! It lives!"

Madeline pointed them both down with a ladle and served up two hearty scoops onto plates. They'd eat it, alive or dead, like it or not. Not like there was much else to eat. Most of the restaurants in town closed down, but all the bars stayed open. Booze was just easier to keep long-term than fish filets or pork chops.

The drone of a radio on the kitchen table, one which was busted open and hardwired to work with vacuum tubes and dangerously conductive custom wiring, served as the background for the family dinner. If the winds shifted a certain way, or a solar flare erupted millions of miles away on the Sun, the radio would change stations automatically. So it did.

"The prices of corn and wheat," the announced drolled, "are expected to reach yet another milestone in the slump. Future markets look to the Iowa index for hope, but recent changes made in the House of Representatives have imposed stern restrictions causing farmers to -." It fell into static intermittently, but the content was the same. A bit of hopelessness and despair. Perfect mood music for their new take on a chicken melt.

"Honey," Madeline said, "we gotta go over some things after supper, so stick around-"

"The market dropped 17%. Coupled with a decrease in federal crop subsidies, it puts you in a hole roughly over 20% on the farm loans."

Jimmy looked at Brandy with shock. "How does she know this?" Madeline was just as surprised. So he turned to his daughter. "We are just fine young lady, thank you. Don't you worry, your pretty little head."

"She also wants to tell you this was the last year for crop subsidies, and unless you're selling short, you can't make the mortgage. You don't have money in the market right now, so there it is-."

"Hey," Madeline interrupted, "how about a little more eating

Brandy turned fully to her father and pointed her spoon at him. "You need another crop with a greater ROI... a greater retail value...corn and wheat aren't getting it anymore....think outside the box."

Jimmy squinted, trying to see through the fog of her words. "Arouai? Is that some...kind of old Navajo word?"

"It's letters, Dad," she said.

He nodded, and turned to nod at Madeline. He knew letters.

Numbers, too. Some of them.

"You guys don't have a clue what I said, do you?"

Jimmy and Madeline turned against her, dipped their spoons in her culinary concoction, and held them up to her mouth.

"Eat!"

Just like old times. She was always a sassy child. It all went downhill when she learned how to talk.

Chapter 3

The sun dropped down to the horizon and sank into the unseen ocean. It was evening. It took Grandpa Elbert that long to get across town, but he was there. His tractor took up both of the handicap spots outside of the only bar with enough business to keep its lights on reliably.

The sign-out front was tampered with in the exchange. Part of the 'n' was scrubbed off and painted over, leaving the rest of the lettering intact. Queers. An old stomping ground under new management.

At 100 years old, Grandpa Elbert was just a bit faster on his feet than he was on his tractor. His legs swung out wide and left his parts to dangle in his pants, like an old cowboy walk or like he had rickets. His back was just slightly curved, in much better shape than someone who sits reading a computer screen or phone all day, every day.

He was scruffy from time to time, but this was an occasion he was clean-shaven with a dab of old spice. He wore a wide brimmed hat indoors. He sported a plaid shirt under his overalls - which made him match with some of the clientele.

He shuffled up to the bar and took in the sights. The decor had changed. A ton of California Prop 64 fliers and campaign posters from years gone by hung around the walls.

A newspaper page was enshrined in glass which showed the headline of the legalization of gay marriage in California. Half the women in the bar had short hair and stern, strong features, and the other half were uniquely pretty with a sharp sense of doll-like fashion.

Grandpa whistled for the barkeep. She turned with a strange glare in her eye.

"Yoo-hoo!" he bellowed. She strode over to him, her thick Doc Martins thudding on the floor.

"Yeah, what?"

"Yoo-hoo!"

She got right up close to him.

"You got my attention - what do you want?"

He did a drinking motion with his hand and jiggled his Adam's apple up and down his throat. "A Yoo-Hoo."

She got it. "Wouldn't you rather have an Ensure? They taste the same."

"En-sure gives me the shits!" he said with a slap on his knee. "That's why I like Yoo-Hoo."

She rolled her eyes. "I can put some Hershey's syrup in a glass of water."

"No, that ain't the same," he said with a very knowledgeable disappointment.

"We serve hard liquor," she explained, "to women who want to get drunk, laid or both!"

"Laid," he stroked his chin. "I like the sound of that! I'll have a sarsaparilla."

She turned away in a huff to go to the backroom where she held her ingredients - not drinks, just drink-adjacent things, like sodas and mixes. Grandpa turned away and examined the playing field he had. All girls, just the way he liked it.

"Tonight's ladies' night, by the look of it, isn't it?"

He turned to the woman in the seat next to him, a sharp-blonde-haired woman with feathered bangs and a nose piercing.

"Every night is ladies' night at Queers," she said.

"This used to be Queens," he complained. "A place where a man could score."

"Well, handsome, you're just one letter and one chromosome off."

Grandpa mulled her words and rolled his jaw like he had some gum stuck behind his dentures that he just couldn't get out. "Would you like to try knocking some boots together?"

She tittered at him. "That is a tempting offer." He waggled his bushy eyebrows in a smooth, wavy motion. Like two worms synchronized their crawl. Then a big, butch woman, a lumber jane of a lass, came in and sat next to the blonde.

"Beat it, Gramps," she insisted. "Go find your own."

Grandpa thumbed his suspenders. "Well, I do love a challenge. Are you ladies sure you wouldn't like to…" The large woman gave him a stern, squint-eyed look. "Alright! I know when I'm not wanted." He hopped off the bar stool and surveyed the territory, which looked a might bit more hostile than before.

There was a live band playing some lively Latin dance music. Grandpa got onto the dance floor and started to move. His legs straightened, and so did his back. He moved fast, like a man a third of his age, feeling the heat and groove.

A woman sidled up next to him, a young girl with a half-shave haircut and a Pride shirt. "You're a great dancer!"

"Arthur Miller dance school," he said. "And Saturday Night Fever."

The girls danced around him as he sashayed his way through the crowd. He slid, swooped and scampered all the way up to the stage where a tough, butch singer was laying down a rough Spanish set.

"Step aside, sonny."

He hip-bumped the lady away from the microphone and picked it up. The bar turned on him until he tapped his feet for the band to join and went off on a surprisingly competent, unexpectedly fluent Despacito.

It took a few seconds, but once the chorus hit, the bar was hopping. All the bar patrons, young and old, got up and joined as the band leaned in hard and tore up their own floor with the rhythm and groove of the hot Cuban set.

The bartender returned from her stock-room trip with Sass in hand and sipped at it idly while she watched.

"I gotta stock this Yoo-Hoo drink."

The bar was blazing, lit up, groovy, dank, bodacious, psychedelic - every generation was having a good time.

Then the cops showed up. Local Deputy Sherriff Delbert spotted Grandpa on the stage after he'd whipped off his shirt and twirled it around like a towel. This started a sudden shirts-off wave for the rest of the bar, a gross infraction of public decency.

"Aw shit! It's the filth!" Grandpa Elbert dropped the mic and made an inch-at-a-time run for the back. Delbert walked over calmly, took him by the arm and led him out the front. Fun was over for the night. For him, The girls stayed inside, with their girls out, until the drinks ran out.

"This is poe-leece brutality, son," Grandpa said. "You can't yank a man away from that kind of scene! Liable to stop my damn heart!"

Delbert drove Grandpa back to the Monticeto farmstead. The John Deere tractor had a boot on the back wheel. It wasn't even big enough to reach around the rim. It was basically a plastic clip on a bag of chips.

It was night by the time they got back. Madeline was in the living room on her old, corded phone, talking to her son, when she saw the strobing lights outside. She was sure it wasn't either of them. And she hadn't seen Grandpa all day. So she put the two and two together.

"I have to let you go, hon," she said. "Delbert is here again. Can't wait to see the two of you. Be safe. Love you." She kissed the phone extra loud and hung it up with a lipstick mark over the receiver. She got up just as the doorbell went off. She opened the door to see Delbert and Grandpa.

"Land's sake, Dad! What am I to do with you? Where have you been? I thought you were in your room."

Grandpa shrugged his way out of Delbert's guiding hands. "Where's a fat ass?"

"His ass is not fat," she retorted defensively. "Just a little

15

portly," she admitted candidly.

"Are you kidding me? He has elephantiasis of the ass. It's the land that time forgot between those cheeks." He turned back and glared Delbert down, pinching his fingers together. "I was this close to getting laid."

Delbert shook his head. "He drove the tractor into town again. You'll have to come by the bar and pick it up."

"I'll go and get it -." Grandpa began. He was cut off when Madeline pointed him up to his room. He rolled his eyes so hard his head leaned back. "Fine, send fat ass! I'm gonna watch Ronald Reagan give the State of the Union address again. Now he was a real President!"

The two younger Monticetos rolled their eyes. Just before Grandpa was out of sight, he gave Delbert the finger behind Madeline's back, then slipped down the hall.

Just another day/night in Hephzibah, where the fastest times came on the back of the slowest tractors.

Chapter 4

Hephzibah was far, far away. Far from anything and far for everyone. The Monticeto Farm was just a spec on the spot in the overlooked dustbin of a remote part of what some people might not even remember to be part of the same country.

Getting flights to and from was complicated. The only way to arrive by air was skydiving. Or getting a connection to Los Angeles and driving the distance.

That was the plan for the sons of the homestead owners. Jimmy and Madeline's sons were on a plane, a small economic one, that was planned for an immediate and swift departure to the bigger city. B.J. and Hammer, identical twins, except for B.J.'s sexual preference, were in shared seats waiting for departure. The seatbelt sign was on and flashing. The plane was already preparing to taxi.

And Hammer was on the phone, screwing up the plane's electronics.

"Mom," he whispered, "I didn't do anything to him. He's here of his own free will. Gotta go bye." He tapped his phone and looked up to the glaring eyes of the rest of the passengers. B.J., meanwhile, rustled his hands in the shallow pockets of his Daisy Dukes.

Ding! The overhead speakers came on.

"Sorry for the delay, folks," the Captain spoke, "but we seem to have weight issues."

"Don't we all, honey," B.J. replied.

Hammer gave him a light slap on the shoulder. "Shut up!"

B.J. changed his pant search to his shirt and pulled out a small vape pen.

"You know you can't vape here," Hammer said.

"You know I get nervous on airplanes!" B.J. hushed.

"So," the captain continued, "we need volunteers willing to take a later flight so we can reduce our weight."

The boys looked out their window to see a big burly handler tossing luggage out of the plane without care onto a portable conveyor truck, where it rolled down to two more unloaders who tossed the bags through a hula-hoop they set up and cheered when something sank through.

A few drug-sniffing dogs paced around erratically with their noses high and tails wagging at some particularly garish-looking luggage. Seemed like they were already making the decisions.

Hammer pressed the call button to report the event.

"Ah," a nearby flight attendant said. "We have our volunteers! Let's all give a big hand to the gentlemen in seats 23a and 23b."

The passengers and flight crew all clapped. B.J. slowly

slipped his vape pen back into his pocket and laughed nervously.

"I - I don't think so," he said.

"We weren't volunteering," Hammer said. "We were - ."

"Too late."

"Thank you so much!" the flight attendant cheered. "Your luggage has already been removed from the plane."

"No!" B.J. protested.

"Yes!" she replied.

"No!" Hammer objected.

"Yes!" she resounded.

"No!" the brothers shouted.

"YES!" the passengers, flight crew, and captain over the speaker said. Hammer looked back. He thought he heard the luggage crew shouting them down too.

They did. All three were looking up, incensed to get on with their game.

Two bulky dudes picked the brothers up from their seats and manhandled them all the way out of the plane, back to the terminal. B.J. grinded himself against the Air Marshall's leg to get something good out of the humiliating experience. Hammer was too upset. He didn't want to get off – by punching a federal agent.

But there was no use. They were tossed back into the airport. And then, four TSA agents immediately swooped in to process them. It was a bust. They were photographed - B.J. took more than one to best capture his good side - and fingerprinted.

"This isn't the kind of prince I normally finger," B.J. complained.

"Subject may be withholding evidence," an agent said. "Prepare for a cavity search."

B.J. looked excited.

"On…the other one, first," the agent said.

"Oh, please," Hammer said, "he needs it way more than me."

One uncomfortable search later - for the agents, not the brothers - the process was complete, and they were given the full dose of industrial-strength hand sanitizer from behind the aptly named NO FLY desk.

An agent, a wide Hispanic woman in her 30s, spoke as she typed in a fast hunt-and-peck style. "Under article 7 subsection 215 of the Homeland Security Act, you are hereby prohibited from using a commercial flight for travel for the designated period of …," she looked up at them and their hopeless, nervous grins, "...whenever we feel like."

She took a red stamp and punched it into their paperwork. It was official. They were as dangerous to the airways as international terrorists and peaceful protestors across the country.

The woman slid the papers forward and walked through a door to an office. She slammed the door, and the force of the wind made the papers drift to the floor.

"Well, you too," B.J. said.

"That's telling her," Hammer mocked.

"I can still hear you," the woman said behind the thin door. The boys grabbed their sheets and ran out of the terminal to the connected car rental agency. They couldn't fly, but they had hands and feet and healthy, albeit slightly used, butts. They could just drive home and dump the car at another airport for them to deal with.

They got their luggage, which looked as equally molested as they were, and a car. A car. A white Range Rover with a stuck back seat door, a conspicuous hole in the passenger seat and no working heater. But the outside looked gorgeous. It was polished and waxed, a showpiece car straight off of the floor. They threw in the luggage and boarded in.

B.J. dialed up home with a sigh.

"Hi, Dad, how are you?"

Hammer looked around the interior to see what they were working with and adjusted the mirrors.

"Fine," B.J. went on, "just fine. Friggin dandy, so much fun...Well, I just called to let you know we decided to take a road trip across the country, bonding and all that wonderful horse shit. We will be delayed just a little bit."

Hammer looked at him, wondering if his lie was getting through.

"Uh-huh. Uh-huh. Okaaaay. See you then, Dad." He hung up and gave Hammer a nasty look.

"What'd he say?" Hammer asked.

"Just this," B.J. said, then punched Hammer in the jaw.

"AAAAAGH!" B.J. screamed. Hammer took it, stiff and stern, but B.J.'s hand was raw. Hammer clenched his hands against the wheel, testing his strength. He saw his brother already suffering and laughed it off.

"He said," B.J. continued, imitating his father's slow and lazy drawl, "If it's your brother's fault for getting you kicked off the plane. I would punch him. So there."

Hammer chuckled. "You still punch like a girl."

"Well, duh!" B.J. protested. "You better know how to get to California from here, Mr. Pister."

"Duh," Hammer retorted. "It's south and west. We go west, then south - how hard can it be?"

So the brothers began their errant journey, kicked out of La Guardia and set out in the wilds of New York on their way back to the dusty plains of California where their sunken dirt bowl home awaited, with every destination they could spare to see in between. They went West for a while, as it made sense, but missed all the routes that actually took them reliably South.

After two days of non-stop driving, the boys made a stop in the closest city with a traveler-friendly industry to host them for a night...

Chapter 5

Five men in wife beaters, gold chains, ruined pants, and very nice shoes turned with glaring eyes and hate-seeded stares as a white Range Rover rode through their hood. At the front were two bottoms, two really odd-looking white boys who were not in Kansas anymore. They were in Detroit.

B.J. and Hammer waved to the men as they passed, dazzling their fingers and everything. The men just kept up their glare, unwelcoming them to their part of the city. The poor, run-down and dangerous part, where no one lived so much as they were waiting for the right opportunity to die.

The brothers pulled into a hotel that looked like it had a multi-story fire that was just put out that morning, but those rooms were still up for rent. They picked out one room, to the disgust and revilement of the owner, and settled in for the night to the sounds of sirens and gunshots. None of these were synched up to the TV, which had ESPN, BET and MTV only.

B.J. was curious to see just what was going on outside. He lifted back the curtain and peered through the iron bars to just barely see the Rover in the parking lot, surrounded by men with tools as they peeled one piece of the car away at a time.

"Huh."

The men also dragged a chain from the nearby ice machine and slid down back to the asphalt to hitch it up to the frame of the Rover. It was clear there was chicanery about, so B.J. did the one thing he could think of: he picked up the room phone and called the front desk.

"Sir, there are guys out in the parking lot stripping my car! Call the police!"

"You guys again," the surly, gruff-voiced clerk said. "Sure, no problem, cracker. I'm all over it."

He hung up immediately. Meanwhile, Hammer hop-stepped out of the shower, hair still wet, feeling pretty good.

"What say we go out and let our hair down?" he asked. "Big city means big club scene."

They both stood still as the sound of a machine gun crackled in the distance like a firework.

"Or," B.J. said, "we could just stay in and keep it. I'm exhausted."

"I'm starving," Hammer said. "We -."

"Can order a pizza. Brilliant, great idea. Please, you don't wanna go out there."

Hammer shrugged and rolled his eyes. His brother. Wimpy, girly little B.J. Always the bottom, never the bride. He fastened on

25

some pants, slipped on his shoes, and went outside to check out the vending machines. B.J. held his breath. Hammer was back in a few seconds. His hair stood on end, and a greasy sweat undid part of his just-done cleansing.

"Pizza?" B.J. said.

"Pizza!" Hammer exclaimed.

Somehow the pizza guy got there unscathed. No surprise- he was also packing. And he had a co-driver. After that bad luck lot, the boys woke up to a car with no wheels, with an extra chain hooked to an ice machine, with no doors or steering wheel, and all the personal effects they kept in the trunk were obviously gone. But they still had the clothes on their backs - purely optional for them - and the money in their wallets. And the car service card so they could get AAA to fix up their car while they checked out. It wasn't even their car, anyway.

B.J. and Hammer went back to the desk. The same clerk was there from last night, still in his chair behind bullet-proof glass like he never left. Which was smart, considering what happened on his watch.

"I noticed," B.J. said, "the police didn't come last night. Great service, right Hammer?"

"Didn't call 'em," the clerk said. "The Po-Po don't come

round here now, no mo'. You boys are on your own. Know what I'm saying?" He punched, literally finger-punched, a receipt printer that slid out a bill. "Da bills $118, cash only!"

"Hundred eighteen!?" Hammer exclaimed. "The sign says sixty! Wait one damn minute. Maybe we ain't gonna pay; what do you think about that?"

"I'm with you, Brother," B.J. said. They stood shoulder to shoulder to combine their posture. They were healthy young men, fit for clubbing and being attractive meat for the scene. The clerk stood up, six-foot-six and five foot wide at the shoulders, an out-of-season linebacker, and walked through the side door, which he had to duck under to pass through.

"Cash! Sure!" B.J. exclaimed. "Cash work for you, Tom?"

"Sure, Jim," Hammer nodded. "Absolutely - we would love to pay cash."

"All of it," the clerk demanded. The boys got their wallets out only to have them snatched away and pilfered appropriately. They stood and smiled as it happened. Then they had to wait. An hour later, AAA finally finished with their job, and the repairman was still laughing. The wheels were a size or so too small, and they had two folding chairs set up in place of their stolen seats, duck taped to the floor.

"What kind of idiot stays here?" the technician said through his chuckles. "Wow! You'd have to be brain-dead or something -."

"Shut up!" the brothers chided.

The technician left, still smiling and silently laughing to himself. His co-driver was laughing hysterically and spread that laughter back to his coworker as they took off. The boys were left with their hopeless car still in the midst of a hostile city. It was a challenge to drive, but it drove. The crooks never touched the engine. They had all the time to take it, or at least take it apart. Gas was still brimmed, too.

What made the drive an extra challenge was having no doors to lean their arms on, no side mirror to check traffic, and the ice machine was still hitched to the tow and rattled behind them as they punched holes in the asphalt wherever they went, which they did not notice immediately.

Not until the unthinkable happened.

Mr. Middleton, a distinguished and genteel Black man, a regular American gangster, and his hulking cohort Bruiser Brasi, stepped out of a suit and tie restoration shop. He held up and admired his brand new tie in the sun, the veneer of the uniquely dyed ink, a perfect royal blue made from the finest silks reflecting the old colors of Middle Eastern kings. A suit fit for Detroit's high and mighty mob boss.

He looked as a rickety Range Rover tore down the road and watched as the wild flail attached to its rear swung hard on a whip-like turn and crashed through the driver's side window of a sleek, shiny black Lincoln Continental. It stuck in for a moment and yanked out, tearing the windshield a little as well, then bounced and ricocheted after the Rover as it merged into the streets toward the freeway out of Detroit.

Mr. Middleton was stunned. He calmly folded his tie and tucked it into his Savile Row suit jacket pocket.

"Was that my Dropbox?" he asked.

Bruiser nodded. "Don't worry, boss. I got da plate."

"Well," Middleton nodded, "isn't this just special."

He started a laugh, deep and booming, like rolling thunder. The car door fell off and clattered in the street. His laugh changed into a low, warbling, sobbing cry instead.

The Monticeto boys were out of town within the hour, none the wiser to what they'd done, but just wizened up while on a rural highway branching the westbound interstate with the southbound highways to their straggler. They slowed down just as the ice box hit its last dent in the road, and the chain broke. The boys ran back to check the status of their vagrant ride-a-long and to unhitch it before someone got hurt.

"I've heard of ghetto ingenuity before," B.J. said, "but this is…"

Inside the ice machine was an Igloo cooler. Nothing else. It was a hollow shell for serving ice that just happened to have an ice box inside of it.

"Look on the plus side," Hammer said as he tapped the lid to a hollow think. "Free cooler."

"Now we just need some beers," B.J. said.

"And we've got a party on wheels!" Hammer said excitedly.

Never once to suffer a bad time for long, the boys loaded the cooler in the back seat - on the floor, the seats were gone - and left the ice machine on the side of the road with the chain wrapped around it.

Chapter 6

The Dirty Sanchez Pas Gay Rodeo. The Dirty on the sign was painted a little off-kilter as an afterthought but artfully done with a cursive swing. The Monticeto sons were on their tear across the country through Oklahoma. It was their last pit stop before the great plains really opened up to the great, wide-open nothing and the last bit of flair they might get to see for several hundred miles.

It was a veritable hoedown of fancy men in cowboy attire. Chaps were mandatory, but pants were optional - clearly. It was leather and jean daddies for miles. B.J. was thrilled. Hammer was respectful, but he was doing most of the driving and was just glad to be off the road for a bit. He needed to recuperate.

B.J. immediately found a man who was unattended with a thick, strong mustache to cozy up next to. Meanwhile, Hammer went to the nearest Cantina to try and forget the bad times, so only the good was left in the back of his brain. The Cantina was a tractor-trailer set up to look like an old-style saloon, part of the on-the-go rodeo tour experience. It was a little stuffy, but sweat was part of the aesthetic. It was a plus.

The first seat he found was next to a decent-looking man. He had a participation badge on his shirt, the name of Casey, showing he was part of the staff or entertainment. He was one of the few people wearing regular jeans and an unopened shirt. He looked downright hetero, a chisel-jawed broad-shouldered boy-faced man, muscled and tanned from real rodeo work.

"How are you doing, sir?" Hammer asked.

"Great, and you?" Casey said. "Don't you just love these little events?"

He had the cutest drawl. Nothing like the folks of Hephzibah, the bastard mix of deep-state Alabama and valley girl confusion. He was a Brokeback boy.

"Yeah," Hammer agreed. "More fairies than you can shake a stick at."

Casey composed himself after the remark and gave a polite smile in response. "I was thinking the same thing myself. Sounds like you're a man after my own heart, brother. Casey's the name."

"Hammer."

Casey raised his hand for two drinks. Hammer got his Miller Genuine Draft and gave a toast to his modest friend. As the evening grew into night, the rodeo raged. The main events were coming to pass. The cowboys were riding - also, there were horses and bulls aplenty. Also, some folks were riding said animals, on their backs, for sport. A lot of different activities were underway outside the trailer, but Hammer sat firmly until he couldn't feel his own self-awareness biting at his back.

Casey stood up from the bar. He was unaffected by the booze and invited Hammer to follow him. Hammer had his eyes half-drawn and was already moving to keep his balance in a perfectly still chair - so he was about halfway to where he wanted.

"I bet you've never seen how the rodeo works from behind the scenes?" Casey said.

Hammer nodded and bobbled his head a bit. "You're not gonna....you know?" He put up his hands to do an insert-screw gesture but missed.

Casey chuckled. He did a little fairy flap. "Do I look like one of those little...?"

He glanced past Hammer, who was chuckling with his head down. The bartender slipped a paper sleeve of powder into the beer, which kicked up a new head of foam and fizz.

"Hey?" Casey said. "Come on. This is a thing of beauty, my friend. Pure beauty."

Hammer shrugged. He picked up his drink and finished it off. He followed Casey in a woozy gait. Things started to kind of change around Hammer. He wasn't so much moving as the world was coasting him along on a private ride without wheels. Things melted past him; the scenery changed in an instant, blurred together, like the after-image of a TV channel left behind after changing to a new one.

SCOTT KINDRED

Meanwhile, B.J. was in the stands. He fully adapted to the setting and swapped out his shorts for long chaps and clean underwear to cheer with the crowd. It was an animal kingdom showdown: Bulls vs Bears. Heavyset, swarthy men riding on the back of horny beasts of burden.

Casey led Hammer into the bull chute, a real behind the scene look where riders were loaded up and mounted for their runs. He guided him past the gate. Hammer took a few steps forward, each one to catch himself from falling flat over until his face was parallel to the ground. He swung his body up and looked as the gates closed. Then the headrush blacked him out.

When he woke up, he looked at his hands. They were swollen, puffy and all white. His arms were covered with multi-colored bruises, a whole pride parade of striped strips that ran up to his shoulder. His chest was similarly abused, with a little leather jacket that cinched under his armpits too snug to be fashionable. He had chaps, but no pants, boots without socks, and was beset by a piercing headache.

He figured out what was going on. He'd been clowned. Thoroughly, utterly tapped upon. He looked around and heard a sharp whistle over the sound of his tinnitus. It was Casey, sitting next to, and leg straddled over the lap of, the bartender.

"Just me and the fairies here," he said, with a nod to his

partner. "Say hello to my husband."

"Hello," Hammer greeted. He snorted and took in a noseful of a truly awful odor. Like pool cleaners that didn't do a good enough job. "Oh God, what is that smell? Where are my clothes?"

"That smell," the bartender said, "is cow estrus, handsome!"

"Cow estrus! You mean cow piss!"

"I like you, darlin'," Casey said, "but Mozart back there really likes you. And that is a big problem if you know what I mean."

Hammer turned. His eyes caught the glare of two glowing red hate spheres in the dark locked up behind a gate which two men were on either side of, poised to open it. A way out opened first, a gate to the open arena space, as Hammer's signal to go.

"Hold on there; we may have gotten off on the wrong foot. I love fairies; my brother is one!" The bull didn't seem to take kindly to that. Of all the things to bring to a gay rodeo, they brought in an animal that probably opposed most Civil Rights legislation. "Oh, shit!"

Hammer ran for it with the bull not far behind. He was a spectacle of the bull ring in an instant, the gayest clown on the show with the meanest bull hot on his perfumed trail.

"I do believe Mozart is in love," the bartender called. "Ain't love grand?" He and his husband laughed raucously and were drowned out by the cheering crowd.

Hammer was in full sprint into the bull ring. Mozart leaped the short wall to cut its path down. The crowd gasped at the monster's tenacity. Its hanging rod nearly clipped the wall off. It was mad and horny and pointed all three of its horns toward Hammer. They squared off with a silent crowd, uncertain of the outcome.

"If I'm gonna die here, then let's go. Come on. Come on, you ugly son of a…"

The bull tilted its head to gauge the distance, then blasted forward on a charge.

"Oh, crap!"

Hammer ducked and dove out of the way. He landed in a roll, got on his feet and ran to the other side as the bull's horns splintered the wood where Hammer once stood.

"OLE!" the audience cheered. Hammer looked up at the audience with a discouraging look on his face, blocked by the overdrawn, happy makeup. He tried to wave them quietly again as the bull wrenched its horns from the wall to make another charge.

"Go bull!" B.J. shouted. He couldn't recognize his own brother in mortal peril.

Not until Hammer signaled to B.J. specifically. Their own brotherly code of unspoken danger. B.J.s jaw dropped when the realization hit him. He hopped off his seat and ran for the railing. Watching in panic and confusion.

Hammer ran toward the arena as the bull charged once more. He dove away in the reverse direction, which sent the bull's shoulder crashing into the rail. B.J. mounted it just in time to get shaken off and fell butt-first down onto Mozart's back. The bull had a higher priority now. It bucked and ran around in a blind sprint through the arena toward one of the gates. The men working the latches dove away as the bull tore through the metal grating. Hammer ran after them all the way into the parking lot.

B.J. steered the bull as best he could with heel kicks and jerks of its ears. It bellowed loud as they crossed through the light-strewn grounds toward the car park. B.J. could have sent it into the side of a truck or across the road to an open field. He could have if he had tried.

The only car that was in their way that the bull could see was a mostly white, slightly remodeled, basically good, used rental Range Rover. The bull lowered its head and pierced the bumper. B.J. was tossed off from the sudden stop and rolled off the hood of the car, leaving two distinct and supple imprints in the metal where he landed.

"No! Not my car! Not again!" B.J. shrilled. The bull ripped the bumper off and pranced away, unable to adjust to the new weight on its head. Hammer ran up and got B.J. off the ground first. A news crew followed, who left the stands when the action proceeded out of the ring.

"That was amazing!" Hammer exclaimed. "Are you okay?"

The brothers locked arms and stood up together.

"They have face painting here?" B.J. asked.

A crowd came pouring from the bull ring, led by Casey. The bull was scratching the fender over its horns against the side of the trailer saloon to pry it off.

"Quit scratching up my paint!" the bartender shouted.

Mozart huffed loud. Its red eyes turned on the audience.

"Uh oh," B.J. said. "I don't think he's happy."

"No one likes being made a clown of," Hammer said. He reached up and wiped off what prosthetics and makeup he could. The news crew watched as the bull charged the audience, now with a much wider profile that was impossible to dodge. The audience split away, leaving Casey as the only one in Mozart's path. Their chase was ended by a shrill, girly scream that echoed into the night.

The bull, satisfied, stood victorious. It was the first case of a bovine-based vehicular accident in at least 100 years.

Chapter 7

The rodeo closed early that night. No late-night parties or half-clothed man-saddle riding tournaments. The night schedule was scrapped as police and paramedics arrived to deal with the bull gone wild. The report was made on the scene, featuring gruesome shots of Casey and his broken ass and the two stand-out stars of the show next to their demolished Range Rover.

The local reporter stood with her microphone tilted between her and the brothers. "You are a hero. You save that man -."

"My brother," B.J. said. "Hammer." He swung his arm around Hammer's shoulder. Hammer did the same and gave him a pat on the shoulder, leaving a smear of his clown paint behind.

"You saved your brother, Hammer's life. You're a hero!"

B.J. rolled his eyes. "I mean, I guess so. I saw an opportunity to have a wild ride - you know what I mean? And then I saw the bull chasing my brother, so I had to change my plans."

"I heard," Hammer mentioned, "you, distinctly, cheering for the bull."

B.J. paused. "Uh - that's because I wanted to use reverse psychology. And give you some motivation. You know?"

"I don't think bulls are susceptible to psychology," Hammer said. "At least not the spoken kind. They're into this kind -." He wiped one of the wetter parts of his clothing and shoved a face-full of cow estrus into B.J.'s face. The brotherly spat and ensuring slap-fight was captured on local news and uploaded to YouTube.

Which was then seen by millions who shared the same sibling rivalry bond and gay pride that the brothers showed. The interview proceeded unseen, with most of the views coming from clips of them bickering or clips of the actual chase and subsequent fender-wearing bull plowing its way through the field of rodeo enjoyers.

The brothers had their information taken by the local state police department to cover them legally from any wrongdoing. And their names, as well as their hometown, were added to the post-production report.

That was seen by gay rodeo, gay culture and gay pride enthusiast Milton Middleton. Son of notorious Detroit mob boss Mr. Middleton, who rode together in the back of a very recently repaired Lincoln town car.

"Is that who I think it is?" Mr. Middleton asked.

"Can we go to a gay rodeo next time they swing by?" Milton asked.

"You don't need my permission, son," Mr. Middleton said. He laid a cherishing hand on his son's shoulder. "I support you and will be proud of who you are and what you do. So long as you can afford it on your allowance."

"Aw, Dad," Milton said, exasperated. His father wagged a finger to placate him. Milton turned back down to his iPad and browsed the rest of the clips in his feed. Mr. Middleton leaned forward to Bruiser, his acting chauffeur.

"Chart a course to Hephzibah, California," he said. "Our *drop* will be waiting there."

"We drivin' or flyin'?" Bruiser asked.

"We'll go by what the wind decides," Mr. Middleton said mysteriously. He leaned back into his seat, arched his fingers, and laughed. His son laughed, too - at a funny cat video.

As for the brothers, they went on their merry way and headed on a clean break out west. Being surrounded by cowboys and chased by a mad bull soured them on traveling through the rest of the southwest. They'd go west first until they hit California, familiar turf, and then head south. Less Republican states in their way. B.J. was a recognized gay hero. He had like a week's worth of fame - and infamy - to wear off.

They drove day over day through Colorado and through the unchecked, churchless corners of Utah and finally crossed the Rockies to hit northern California on a country road. There were trees everywhere, enough to block their signals.

"Anything?" B.J. asked.

"Maybe if we," Hammer said. He moved his arm up while B.J. was forced to move his leg down. The two were tangled up on the roof of the car, striking a balance between not falling off and reaching high enough to break through the shroud of missing phone waves. They got a bar here and there but nothing solid and could only get the right angle by holding one another in a Twister-style mix-up. "Yeah, that's it. Yes, that's it - yeah - yea -."

They got something, and the light from their phones shone down on a farmer who seemingly appeared out of the bush. He had a thick, untouched grey beard but no mustache, a straw hat and a stern expression. And a shotgun.

"No, no," B.J. said.

"What say thee," the stranger asked, "why ye be here in these neck-of-the-woods consorting in this sort of manner?"

"Is that Swahili?" Hammer asked. "Or maybe German?"

The farmer aimed his gun up at the boys. "The Devil hath many a wicked way heathen. Vile animals."

"Heathen?" B.J. repeated. "No, you don't understand we're brothers, we love each other."

CLICK-CLICK

The boys hopped down fast and boarded their car. B.J. wrapped around into the driver's seat while Hammer came in head-first through the window.

"Step on it!" Hammer shouted.

The farmer shot out the back window, then with his second barrel, shot again. Their bumper - recently repaired - popped right off, leaving their number plate behind as well.

They had to stick to the uninhabited roads. No cities or touring, no stops at major metropolitan areas. And they couldn't trust the backwoods of California at night. No LA district, no hookups on highways along the West Coast. They doubled back into Nevada and took a quick sprint through the desert.

And into Reno.

Reno didn't really count as a city. It was more of a kitschy place to get some gas and food and not be asked too many questions. It was the storm drain spill off of Vegas. No narcs in sight, and surprisingly, their car wasn't the worst one on the road that was still street-legal.

They got supplied up and headed down onto Interstate five for the last stretch to Hephzibah. It was blistering hot all through the desert. That didn't get fixed as they drew closer to home. It was starting to look a little more familiar. The desolate, flat horizon. The burnt-brown texture of the ground. The depleted fields of wasted crops. The gay bar. They were home.

All that was left was the final drive down Route 45 and a turn-off on the unmarked dusty dirt road that led to Monticeto Farms. They were so happy they couldn't help themselves but dance, so they shoved the Rover into a low gear, locked the wheel and let it coast while they "Kiki" danced beside it all the way up to the house.

It was a celebration.

Chapter 8

Madeline was in the kitchen nook preparing large trays of party foods. She had dry hotdog buns basted lightly with seasoned vinegar and topped with specially cut hot dog sausages, with garnishing of edible weeds plucked from the yard. On another tray were deviled eggs, but the topping had been spiced so much it looked orange and had a clumpy consistency. She had a nut platter as well, buttered bread sticks covered with chopped nuts and then glazed with a film of honey.

"Brandy," she called, "why don't you join the family in the barn? I'm almost done here."

Brandy was coloring with crayons at the table in an electric schematics book, linking up all the missing circuits. "Mom, you know I don't do well with the inbred."

"You ain't allergic to bread," Grandpa said. He had a two-story house of cards going on. His hands were dead still. He had to check them periodically to make sure there was still circulation within them. And when there wasn't, he sat on them until they warmed back up.

He caught something approaching out of the corner of his eye. "What the hell is that?" He saw it coming out of the nook window.

"Looks like a tornado!" Brandy exclaimed.

"What honey?" Madeline craned her head toward the window and saw a plume of slow-moving dust approaching with some dark shade covered in the center. "Oh, my stars!"

The strange phenomenon continued on at a steady pace until it hit a slope. Then it sped up. The mystery object in the middle was matched by two strangely gyrating, wobbling figments beside it.

"Jimmy!" Madeline called. Jimmy ran in and looked out the window.

"What the hell is that?" he said.

"Looks like a tornado to me," Brandy said.

"A tornado?" he repeated. "Here?"

"No, dumb ass," Grandpa said. "It just looks like one."

"Come to think of it," Brandy mentioned, "the current barometric pressure is all wrong."

"It's the aliens," Grandpa said. "Got to be. Come to reclaim their saucer that crashed here aught-all years ago."

"There's no such thing as aliens," Jimmy protested.

"The Fermi Paradox would argue otherwise," Brandy said.

The cloud grew closer and closer, and the figures grew more erratic even as the thing in the center stayed steady and constant in its pace. Finally, some of the dust broke away as the crowd exceeded the speed of the dust off the ground.

"Oh, my stars!" Madeline yelled. "It's the boys!"

B.J. and Hammer finally broke out of the dust cloud, which covered them in a layer of dirt. They did their best to shake it off while Katy Perry cheered them on from the radio. Madeline ran out of the house with the rest of the family following. Jimmy, in his rush, ran hip-first into the table and knocked over the nearly finished house of cards.

"Sorry, Grandpa!"

"You did that on purpose!" Grandpa shouted. "Sabotaging son of a -."

A wind from the door knocked the rest of the cards to the floor. The family ran out to the barn, where the welcome party was all setup. B.J. and Hammer fell back into the dust trail as their best dance moves weren't capable of keeping up with the Rover on its way down the slope. But they didn't think it was prudent to run up and hit the brakes or unjam the wheel.

The barn was done up with a banner and tables of food, seats for sitting and family for meeting. The Monticeto family was gathered up to welcome home the wandering sons once more. It was a calm, polite little reunion of a scattered clan of failed farmers and local fixtures to the town's demographics. Delbert was there acting as a warden to keep everyone happy and all surprises well-contained. He heard a blaring radio outside and opened the door to see what commotion was coming.

The Range Rover bore down on him like a runaway boulder. He shut the doors.

"Run for your lives!" he called. "The boys are back in town!"

The dozen-plus party guests paused for a moment, then realized he was serious. He yanked the doors open as wide as he could, with a cousin helping him on the other side. All the young and elderly guests hobbled out and spread out away from the barn as the Rover continued its speed up the slope. The boys gave a futile chase to catch up to it before the inevitable happened. Delbert dove out of the way as the Range Rover plowed its way into the barn, knocked away tables and crumpled plastic chairs and then burst through the rear wall, where it hit some air and jostled the wheel free on landing. The car turned sharp and front-ended the tree next to the pond in the back.

The family turned up just in time as the car crashed through to save the refreshments table and stood by as the boys ran in to survey the damage following the sound of metal crunching against sturdy wood.

"We needed a back door anyway," Brandy said.

Madeline saw her boys and ran over with her arms out to hug them. "You're home!"

"Kill anybody on the way?" Grandpa asked.

The brothers exchanged looks. The rest of the guests huddled back in and shouted, "Surprise!". B.J. and Hammer shared hugs with friendly relations, got a stern but glad head shake from cousin Delbert, and set aside their brief adventure to bask in the warmth of good family life. Jimmy strode up to his sons, which put the two on a semi-defensive stance, having been responsible for the additional, not up-to-code, doorway. Jimmy wrapped his arms around both of them, which tensed them up and put the boys at ease at the same time. "Thank God you're both alright!" "Yeah, Dad, it was quite an adventure!" Exclaimed Hammer. B.J. just grinned sheepishly and nodded. "Well, I want to hear about it later; right now, I have to go out to the back nine and tidy up the stover," Jimmy said anxiously. "We can help you with that, Dad," B.J. said. "That's fine, boys, but I need to keep busy, or I think about things too much. But I'm mighty glad you're home safe and sound." Jimmy gushed. Jimmy acknowledged his family and left the barn, back to the work that is never done.

The boys were home. The sights and sounds of the cities were behind them. It was just them, the farm, and a totally calm future ahead.

And a car in the field.

And one more out in the corn. Hiding in the withered stalks was a beat-up Lincoln Town Car with a thick, gruff man at the wheel, watching through binoculars. He saw the boys and their disheveled state, the whole family in superior numbers, and the cooler box in the back of the car.

Bruiser moved back in his seat and slowly rolled the car through the field back to town with his report...

Chapter 9

The Canterbury Pub. One of the few fine establishments in the small town of Hephzibah. Just like everything in the farming hamlet, it was a little outdated. The wood on the walls was real, and the paint was real authentic lead paint that chipped off in inopportune overhead places. It was one of the few buildings with reliable Wi-Fi on a satellite that was installed in a lot next door. A classic, old-school wide dish array satellite which had a smaller, modern satellite inside of it. No one knew which one actually worked, so both stayed on constantly.

Mr. Middleton was holed up in there. After arriving in town and seeing that the only available motel looked somehow worse than the ones where he came from, he decided to rent out space in the pub as a VIP. Two old-fashioned rooms, cots and wash basins, where clientele were encouraged to sleep it off, were available. He sipped from a sour glass of wine while he prepared himself for a meeting. He had his laptop, and the charging was adequate, though he did notice the lights flicker when his son plugged his phone into a wall jack. They were operating at threadbare levels but were still floating.

Mr. Middleton got up and took his laptop underarm to set up his meeting in a more accessible room when Bruiser beat him to it and opened the door to invite himself in.

"Got more bad news, boss, you ain't gonna like it none."

Mr. Middleton stepped back and took a calming breath. "I am sure I'll love it. In the theater of the absurd, this would be the perfect time for a gratuitous grin." He smiled and motioned for his man to proceed. Bruiser looked behind him. He was totally lost from the hallway over the threshold.

"They have a big party going on out there," Bruiser explained, "with lots of people. All that and one special cooler. I saw it."

Mr. Middleton nodded with his tempestuous grin. The bathroom door opened up, and Milton appeared with a hair weave and pink robe, sunglasses indoors and punk bunny slippers. He had earbuds in and was humming to the tune of *The Girl from Ipanema* in a falsetto tone. The men watched him go on his way back into the guest room.

Mr. Middleton nodded toward his son. "I would send him out there to watch the place, but being discreet isn't his cup of Earl Gray."

"Who's that?" Bruiser asked. "That's Milton - do we know an Earl?"

Mr. Middleton dropped his smile. And stepped on it. "Go, make sure my Dropbox doesn't go anywhere." Bruiser nodded; simple instructions were best. The boss turned and approached his son. Milton took out his earbuds to hear his father. "*He* wants to speak to us. So wear something…normal."

He left to set up his meeting while Milton was left to wonder what was wrong with what he had on. Mr. Middleton went to a separate room with a prepared cup of Earl Gray of some American brand that chapped his mouth and set up the conference call on the fanciest piece of end table he could collect. The laptop was plugged in, the signal was strong, and the Zoom call was ready to receive the responder.

Milton came in, dressed down a bit. He took his wig off, put on some pajama pants, and replaced the slippers with socks. It was slightly better. It's still a bit garish. Mr. Middleton neglected any comment. The call connected. An older Italian-looking man appeared with slicked-back silver hair and a suit straight out of Armani. His handle was his name: Mr. Giovanni.

"Greetings, Sir," Mr. Middleton said.

"You never call," Mr. Giovani said. "What's this about?"

"You told me," Mr. Middleton said, "you wanted to speak to us…. Don't you remember Don Giovanni?"

Mr. Giovanni looked confused for a moment. "My name is *Lloyd*. You have been watching too many Godfather movies, Monty. And what's with the British accent? You're about as British as I am."

"Am, too," Monty politely pushed back. "Mother's side."

Lloyd shook his head once more and waved his hand in a circle to get on with it. "Where's the evidence I paid for?"

"Let me be breviloquent," Monty said. "The video and the drop-box are missing, but don't you worry, sir, we know exactly where they are."

"If you know where it is, then it can't be missing!" Lloyd snapped.

"Excellent reasoning," Monty said.

"Bravo, sir," Milton added.

"Can it!" the guido demanded. "Get it back. Do what you gotta do, 'cause if you don't do what you gotta do, then I will be forced to do what I gotta do to make you do what you gotta do. Got it?"

"You're telling us to do what we gotta do," Milton nodded along.

"You know, fruit cup, you ain't as thick as I thought you were."

"Fruit cup!?" Milton raised his voice. "Why, you eggplant Parmesan-eating mother-"

Monty slapped his son's mouth shut and held back his

wretched protesting. Milton shifted to a non-verbal offense with his finger. His father kicked his chair away before the boy managed it. Lloyd witnessed the son go crashing out of frame to the sound of a low moan, and his business partner took up the center of the panel instead.

"We'll get it back," he said. "I promise."

"You had better," Giovanni said, "or don't bother to come home. How's that for breviloquent?"

He left the call. Or tried to. It took some doing on his part because he wasn't used to the layout, so Mr. Middleton cut off the call on his end instead.

"What'd you push me for?" Milton asked. He raised himself up to see his father's offending finger stuck up right next to his face. Mr. Middleton beared down on his son with a steady glare of wide, threatened eyes.

"I have seen him break bones for less," he warned.

"Fine, I forgive you," Milton said. He got up and turned to the bar, where an unwilling audience held his position, desperately pretending not to hear anything. "Hey, barkeep, Shirley Temple, please."

"No," Mr. Middleton said. "Take your Shirley Temple to go. Get out there and watch the farm, too. Go!" Milton made a sour face and grumpily got up to go. The rest of the patrons in the seated areas watched him go. It was dinner and a show all of a sudden, but once Milton was gone, they went back to their idle chatter and private meals. Meanwhile, the Shirley Temple arrived a bit too late but came with complimentary accusing glares. "What? It's not mine, really!" The men turned back to their own lives and let Mr. Middleton live out his.

He picked up the drink and sipped at it cautiously as he walked over to the window across the floor of the pub. Across the street was an old, renovated theater with open auditions for Othello. He beheld it with a gentle sorrow and puckered lips...

Chapter 10

After the fever pitch of commotion from the boys' return, the Monticeto farmhouse enjoyed a relaxing, ordinary day. The TV was on as loud as it could go, so much so that a particularly bassy voice or sound shook the plastic frame and distorted the image. The ceiling fan was also on full blast. Air con was expensive, and they couldn't afford an industrial unit. All the dust killed their last window hanger, so the homestead was left to improvise, one way to stay cool in the summer.

Grandpa Elbert sat in his recliner, the only one with ears that needed a TV tuned too high, and grinned mischievously at the weather girl. The things he thought of doing to her. He could wear an all-blue body suit and slip right into the background. She'd be guiding a heated front straight into his crotch and lay a hand on his storm column.

He had thoughts like that, in and out of waking, all day long. The only things that could distract him had to go right in front of his face to register. That was when the family terrier Wag and his partner in pet crime, Cotton, the cat, came into the living room with something from outside. It was never anything good, usually a desiccated critter or a mummified log of its own poop, but something was different this time. It looked green and leafy like something grew out in the field for once. Grandpa got a closer look.

No such luck - it was just a couple of dollar bills. Or were they tens? No, they were hundreds. Grandpa's eyes went wide to the point of bulging a little.

"Come here, baby," he said. He got up and bow-legged his way over, dipping down further with each step. Wag saw him coming and ran for it. "Come on, you little fur-ball!" He stomped after the pair until they went up the stairs and looked down at him tauntingly, knowing it would take him a good half hour to hike his way up there.

"Maddy!?" he shouted. "Where's my shout-gun!?"

Wag seemed to understand the implication and dropped his mouth open. The cash fell out of his mouth to the floor. Wag turned and ran past Cotton - into Cotton and sent the cat tumbling out of the way. Cotton jumped on the banister and away for dear life onto the whirling ceiling fan. The extra draft from its body caused the dollar bills to drift down from above. Grandpa caught one or two, then tried to tongue-catch the third before it fell to the floor, out of his reach. While he did, Cotton spun the ceiling fan into a gear-grinding whir and was flung off into a tassel of flypaper over the window. She fell to the floor and dragged every speck of dust in a clingy trail out the door with Wag.

Madeline finally came in and saw the paper fluttering through the air. She grabbed it from Grandpa just as he bent down past a fifty-degree angle to get it. He had to use his hands on his knees to brace himself back up, and Madeline collected the money from him when it slipped from his fingers. He saw her with his money, rightfully won from the dog's mouth, and put his arms up.

"I'll wrestle you for it," he said. "Best two out of three."

"Not a chance, you old fart."

"I was around when the lady-folk was fighting for their rights. I helped give you your equality, and I'll fight you like any man."

"I'd break you in two by sitting on you," she said. "And where'd it even come from?"

Wag returned, now with even more money in his mouth. Cotton hightailed it in with a few bills stuck to her sticky paper coat. Madeline made a lunge for the cat but missed. She followed Cotton upstairs while Grandpa tried to catch up to Wag. The both of them held their ground as the stampeding continued upstairs. It sounded like the walls were a few steps shy of breaking and caving inward. Wood splintered, and plaster shattered. Grandpa couldn't tell if it was the cat or the woman making all the damage.

Madeline finally chased Cotton back to the stairs. It learned its lesson against flying off with the ceiling fan running, so it scampered down the stairs. Grandpa snapped into view, along with two cold iron barrels of his shotgun.

"Give it up, kitty," he said, "or I'll send you to the great kennel in the sky."

Cotton was undeterred. It hissed and flew past him into the corner, where it finally got stuck on its own yellow coattails. Madeline came down the stairs with some chipped paint in her hair.

"Where's he getting all this money?" she asked.

Hammer, B.J. and Brandy came downstairs to see what the commotion was all about. Thankfully, it wasn't their rooms that were ruined. But they did see the end result of Grandpa holding up a shivering cat covered in dollar bills. Wag stood by to watch or give condolences. Or smugly mock his partner in pet crime.

B.J. brushed Grandpa aside and checked the money. The pets teamed up against him. Cotton hissed, and Wag snapped at him. Grandpa raised the gun in self-defense, but Madeline lowered it for him. Brandy pointed for him to get in there. He gave her the finger and dove for the cat. Hammer took a leap at Wag but missed. Wag ran under him for the door, rammed his head into the frame and dropped the cash on his way out. He kind of sputtered out in the yard and fell on his side, doing donuts in the dirt until he regained his sense of balance.

B.J., Hammer and Grandpa all went for the money and

wound up in a pile.

"This ain't the time nor place, ya idjits!" Grandpa hollered.

"You ain't my type anyway!" B.J. called.

Grandpa bit. His false teeth hurt just like the real things, a rousing endorsement for denturists everywhere. He got Hammer's share. All that was left was avoiding the claws of Cotton in full defense mode, but Wag came back to avenge his fallen feline friend. Or to take some of the money and run away. The men gave chase while Madeline tried to strip Cotton free of the money, only to get a spring trap face full of kitty fur on her head. Brandy ducked under the table to avoid the chaos until her mother wound up running outside to get away from the cash-crazed cat.

They all wound up running toward the pond where the rover crashed the other day. The men changed their angle of approach. Instead of following Wag, they followed the trail of stray bills that laid paw-printed in the dust all the way up to the edge of the water. A small stream formed from the back of the cracked, overturned cooler where the money originated. Damp C-notes poured out from the cooler in the back of the car. Some were picked up by the dog, and the rest went downhill into the water.

The surface of the pond was covered in $100 bills. It was like algae but expensive. Hammer and B.J. leaned to get a closer look while Grandpa dove straight in and paddled for his life to stay above the surface. Brandy returned with her mom, who had some fly paper stuck to her done-up hair and scoffed in the old man's direction.

"Stand up, Grandpa," she said.

Grandpa lifted himself up in the waist-high water and snatched a very waterproofed bill from it. "Well, you know you can drown in an inch of water, little miss know-it-all." He straightened out the bill, held it up to the sun, checked it over for obvious signs of counterfeiting - whether he knew them or not - and smelled it -. "Yahoo! We're rich!"

He started to splash and threw the water, and the money, all over himself. Hammer and B.J. jumped in after him and started to collect the money joyfully. Grandpa swatted them away from the bills on his person.

"No takesies touchsies," he snarled.

"They'll lose all their value attached to you," B.J. protested.

"You'll just spend this on spandex and hand cream," Grandpa fired back.

"Quit being stubborn, the both of you," Hammer insisted. "Just give it -."

Grandpa wound back a wild swing and hit Hammer in the face. The boy flew back and swam his way to shore. He climbed his way out and was ready to dive back in when a sudden, distinctive *click* interrupted them. It wasn't the shotgun. Grandpa left that inside.

Some strangers showed up and held the family at gunpoint. The Monticeto Farm became the ground zero of a hostage crisis.

Chapter 11

Mr. Middleton held his gun on the family. He trained his sights on Hammer first. He seemed like the most able-bodied one out of all of them. Once he surrendered, the rest fell in line, however sheepishly. He was flanked by Bruiser, who was intimidated with his simple, wide-bodied presence and sharp dark suit, and Milton, who was…there and in a reasonable tuxedo and a bit of highlighting makeup with studs in his ears.

"Allow me to introduce myself," Mr. Middleton began. He looked over to the whole family to make sure he had their full attention. "I am the proprietor of that windfall you are bathing with. My name is Middleton."

"Shit!" Grandpa exclaimed. "Does that mean this is his damn money?" He looked at the limp bill in his hand, then to the gangster, then his eyes turned up to Heaven. He went to his knees and sank chest-deep in the water. "God, if you strike him dead and let me keep the money, no more porn..for a week." The family looked up for a moment and stepped back. Mr. Middleton gave a short glance to the sky but saw no clouds, not even white ones.

"Fine," Grandpa said. He snapped his fingers and pointed at the assailant. "Wag, Cotton, Attack!"

Everyone turned to Grandpa once more. The concern over

his mental health before became a full-blown confirmation. Even the animals looked at him in shock and disbelief, like how *dare* he include them. Just to be safe, Middleton lowered his gun to the pets. They went running toward the house, whimpering the whole way.

"Wimps," Grandpa called out. "It was worth a try."

Wag ran at full tilt for cover under the Range Rover, then kept running - but not before snagging just one more thing that fell out of the wreckage. It wasn't a piece of cash money, and it was a slightly wet, waterproof baggie containing something inside. Cotton waited up for him, and they ran inside together to hide.

Mr. Middleton motioned for everyone to come out of the water and away from the pond. "I am afraid I must ask all of you to take this little three-part act inside. Move!" The family started to mobilize. Grandpa had some finger gestures to show, but Madeline kept his arms in check. Brandy was there, too. Her whole mind was centered on protecting the young'uns while she could. Middleton turned to Bruiser as the family hiked up the dusty hill path. "Check it out."

Bruiser went to the cooler and shook it. A clump of soaked bills splatted to the ground, about the same amount that was on the pond. He looked in the cooler. A few bills clung to the sides. He scraped them away and clutched his fingers around a secret slide-away compartment in the bottom, which was empty. He turned and shook his head.

"Collect it up," Middleton motioned. Bruiser nodded and whipped out a garbage bag. He went to Grandpa first to collect. Grandpa scraped the dollar bills off of his body, wadded them up in his hand, wrung them out a little, and then stuck the whole thing down the front of his pants. He rubbed it around like a sponge bath. Middleton turned to his son with a smile.

Milton went over. Grandpa eyed the young man down smugly, certain his strategy would work. But it didn't. Milton reached down and stole the money from him. Then, lingered for a moment. I just kind of hung out until Grandpa was the first to try pulling away. Milton winked as he deposited the cash into the bag.

Meanwhile, Brandy decided to do the smart, yet sassy thing, and record with her iPhone. Her family looked at her like she was insane. Bruiser came around with the bag and shook them all down for the cash they had.

"Where's a fat ass when you need him?" Grandpa grumbled.

The family was forced into the living room. Mr. Middleton and Milton followed in soon after. Mr. Middleton spotted the shotgun and had everyone steer away from it while Milton went to pick it up. He worked it cautiously, like it was his first time playing with such a toy, and made sure it wasn't loaded, but could be in his hands. Everyone went onto the family couch, on which they barely fit. Middleton couldn't find a place that looked dignified enough to sit in, so he stood and continued to hold them all up.

"Is this everyone?" Middleton asked.

Grandpa was seated precariously on the arm of the sofa. He opened his mouth to talk - to tattle - so Madeline whipped him in the rear with a pillow and knocked him over.

"Sorry, Dad," she whispered. "Love you."

"I think so," Milton answered. "There were so many people here the other night it's hard to tell."

Middleton nodded and held them up until Bruiser returned with a wet garbage bag full of the missing cash.

"Forty-nine thousand, two hundred," he said. "We're missing eight hundred."

"You taught that shaved bear how to do math!?" Grandpa exclaimed.

Middleton aimed the gun at Grandpa. The old man settled onto his knees and started praying desperately. Middleton kept the gun on the old man and looked down the row of his hostages on the sofa. "There was a thumbnail drive with this money. Where is it?"

"Thumb*nail*?" B.J. said.

"It is a small device," Middleton explained, "named so for

its approximate size to -."

"We know what it is, jackass," Hammer said. "We got phones, we use computers. We just don't get one here."

"We haven't seen any thumbnail drive," Madeline answered.

Middleton lowered the gun down and pressed it to Grandpa's head. The old man's prayers took on a slightly louder, more pronounced tone of old - possibly real, authentic - Latin. He was old enough to learn it directly from real speakers, after all.

"You want to think about that?" Middleton asked.

"You think we wouldn't tell you if we knew?" she said.

"That depends on how much this wizened old man means to you."

"Which is…" B.J. said, "y'know….quite a lot."

"Would we say quite a lot?" Hammer whispered.

"Pair of ungrateful little- " Grandpa huffed.

Middleton pressed the gun harder to the head until Grandpa tipped back. His spine straightened out and cracked in a place like a reclining chair that got stuck.

"You have twenty-four hours to find it," Middleton warned. "I'll give the person that finds it a grand. Don't fail me, though. It won't go well for you, you Norman Rockwellish nightmare of a family. Return the thumbnail drive to me, and I will be back on the next plane to Detroit. No cops, capeesh?"

Bruiser led the procession out, then Milton and then Middleton with his gun still up. They left with their eyes on the Monticetos all the way up the drive. When they were clear, Middleton turned around.

"Whatever you do, don't take your eyes off any of them. Especially that old man. Got it?"

"Got it!" his cohorts said. They piled together into their local rental, a compact number that barely fit Bruiser and the money bag in the back, and they drove back up the road, just enough to stay on observation for the rest of the day. The Monticetos had a ticking clock. They had to find the thumb drive - wherever it could be - just for a fraction of the miracle money they thought was theirs. All the while, Mr. Middleton had no idea just what he was getting himself involved with....

Chapter 12

Milton and Bruiser were on lookout duty again. They stayed in the cornfield near the farmhouse behind the barn. Their job was to monitor the family in case anything happened. If any of them left, the rest would have to die. If the cops showed up, they'd have to die. Any progress that didn't go towards finding the thumb drive would be a mark of death against them. And if they did find it or give it up willingly, the call would go to them first, and they could drive right up the road to pick it up before the family had a chance of thought or chance to betray them.

It was a perfect little setup. Shame that it was so utterly bland.

One thing of note did happen. Someone else showed up. A new man and evidently a welcome arrival. It was Jimmy, who they failed to recognize was the man of the house. And they had no time to keep eyes on him. They had a priority list, and Grandpa was at the top.

The old coot was styled in a zoot suit fresh out of the 40s, which was ironed, pressed and restored using historical preservation museum techniques to be wearable again. His hair was slicked back, with a dab of Brylcreem, into a tiny, tight ponytail; he was heading out for a night on what little town there was.

On his tractor.

"Where is he going now?" Milton asked.

"How are we going to stop him?" Bruiser asked.

"Just park him in!"

"He'll run us over! He's gotta have a whole two tons over us in that thing."

"We have to think of something. Think, think, think of something, oh my."

"I could whack him. That would stop him for good."

Milton pondered it. He didn't have the same hard edge as his father. "We're just going to have to follow him and see where he goes and keep him out of trouble."

Bruiser nodded and shifted the car into drive. The lights on the tractor went on. Smoke belched out into the barn from the muffler pipe over the engine.

"I think I would rather just whack him," Bruiser said. They bumped and undulated their way out of the dry corn rows and caught up to the road far back from the farmstead. They crawled along the road to get there, and even then, at their slowest, they caught up as Grandpa just barely got his tractor up to speed.

Grandpa leaned back and belted the tune of *Chattanooga*

Choo-Choo while he merged onto the main road, going 15 miles an hour in a 45-mile zone. And Milton and Bruiser were stuck behind him.

"Carefully," Milton said. "He can't know we're tailing him."

"I got it," Bruiser said. "It ain't like he's got no rearview mirror."

They were stuck behind him for 30 minutes as he crept into town. 30 minutes of watching an old man occasionally stand up and gyrate on his seat to dance to music they couldn't hear. 30 minutes of not even really using the accelerator at all, just coasting and drifting a length or so behind. World's slowest car chase.

When they got into town, things sped up a little. The presence of other cars made them feel like being stuck, stop after stop. Behind the tractor was just a normal part of town life with so few major roads. A few intersections got stuffed up from late-night bar-hoppers. There was nothing else to do in town but drink, so every car was in a low-risk DUI zone. A slow car crash was still a crash.

Every driver that drove past Grandpa gave him the finger. Even cars on the other side of the road because his tires went over the double yellow lines. The gangsters followed him onto the outskirts of town to a bar with a lit-up sign that piqued Milton's curiosity. The tractor moved into the parking lot, and Grandpa cut the wheel hard to only take up one handicapped space before he went into *Queens*.

"Oh my," Milton said. "This will be interesting."

Bruiser was more apprehensive. He pulled in and waited to escort the young son of the boss out while Grandpa hopped off and did his best rickety-legged strut into the door.

"Elbert!" the bar all called in unison. Grandpa snapped his snazzy orange-stripe suspenders and tipped his hat before making his way to the bar. Everything was already lit up and active, and it just kept glowing when he arrived. Milton walked through with Bruiser sheepishly in tow.

Grandpa took a seat at the bar, and the bartender slid him a prepared, ice-cold, lick-it-and-you'll-get-stuck Yoo-Hoo. "Thanks, darlin'," he said.

She smiled as he tipped the glass up to his lips and un-parched them. "You're making me rich with this chocolate water. I can barely keep it in stock. Who knew?"

"I did, darlin," he said. He straightened up his bow tie to make it big and wide. Made his neck seem thicker and less saggy. "Any lonesome ladies around tonight?"

"Not many here are on your team tonight, Elbert. But you love a challenge." He raised his glass to her and finished it off for the spring of energy it would provide him.

Milton and Bruiser sat at the bar near the center. It was a mixed crowd. The men hung out with men, and the ladies hung out with ladies. Mixed pairs were there as friends and only flirted with other people. Bruiser and Grandpa were the only straight men there, it seemed, which made the thug perplexed as to why they even showed up.

"Hi, fellas," the bartender called out. "What will it be?"

"I'll have a Midori Collins," Milton said.

"We're still on the clock," Bruiser reminded him.

"Fine," he sighed. "Shirley Temple, please."

While they ordered, Grandpa was on the move. Bruiser caught sight of him on the dance floor. The old man was grooving to the hip-hop track by Big Noyd and Big Twin 'All Pro' on the turntable. It was like his legs were constantly buckling and snapping at the joint, but he recovered and zipped back up just before he hit the ground like a marionette with half its strings in a knot. And he was laying it on with two girls who were just there to dance.

Everything was going smooth, a plain old night out, when the pulsing punk and blue lights were overpowered by strobing blue and red from the front window. Milton caught it out of the corner of his eye mid-sip and reflexively sucked his drink down hard.

"Oh my," he gasped. "We gotta get Gramps out of here before -."

"Before I have to whack him," Bruiser said.

The two got up and ran for the dance floor. They scooped Grandpa up while his back was turned, one for each elbow, and carried him toward the rear exit.

"Who are these ruffians!?"

"We're sorry," Milton said, "but we have to get you out of here before the sheriff arrests you. You don't want to get in trouble now, do you?"

"Hey, I remember you," Grandpa said, snarling at Bruiser. "And I *definitely* remember you. Couldn't get enough the first time?"

They ignored his snippy remarks and chauffeured him to the rear door. Deputy Delbert came in. He was greeted as if he, too, was a regular and waved down or tipped his hat to the patrons in his way. They all just danced around him, dodged him and got out of his way. He went to the bar and tapped for attention.

"What can I get for you?" the bartender asked.

"A dusty old man," he said.

"Never heard of that cocktail. Is there sarsaparilla in it?"

"No, just a big ol' Yoo-Hoo."

She smirked and looked around. "He's wearing a roadwork orange and yellow suit, but if you can't see him, then I don't know."

Delbert sighed. One of his deputy deputies came jogging back to him as some men brushed up against him. "Not in the restroom, sir."

"You sure?" Delbert asked.

The man had a thousand-yard stare - a look that had seen a lifetime of regret in the span of mere seconds. "Yes."

Delbert scratched his forehead. It wasn't like old Grandpa to give up the ghost without a fight, or to skip out without getting rejected enough times, or to leave without making a fool of himself, or to just leave his tractor behind if he felt like the getting was good.

Something else had to be going on at the old Monticeto homestead…

Chapter 13

Right when Grandpa was leaving, Jimmy was coming home. And his evening was a bit dry and dull. He just wanted to get home and relax with the family, see the boys and talk about their trip, maybe have something to eat or find an excuse to get something in town. Grandpa would be there, but otherwise, he was excited for a nice night home.

He opened the door to a shotgun pointed at his face. B.J. was on guard at the door, armed up and ready to defend the homestead with everyone else hiding behind him to back him up and keep the kickback from the gun from flipping him over.

"Make a move, and I'll blow you to smithereens," B.J. said through grit teeth.

Jimmy leaned up to see over the barrel just to make sure it was who he thought it was. "Put the gun down, Marvin. Who was crazy enough to give him that?"

"Dad!" everyone shouted. B.J. lowered the gun happily.

"We thought you were the Mob guys!"

"Mob guys?" Jimmy said. "What are you talking about? Gimme that!" He snatched the gun away, checked the breach, unloaded it and snapped it back together. He pointed to the living room, where everyone immediately went and took a seat. They had some explaining to do. Unfortunately, they were all too excited and started explaining all at once.

"We got kicked off the plane," Hammer said, "and had to drive across the country and went through Detroit -."

"How was I supposed to know he was a mob boss?" B.J. said. "Or that we were hitched up to some kind of rare mobster secret deal?"

"Despite not being a major Italian-American hub for much of the 19th century," Brandy explained, "Chicago became a massive force of continental mafia leadership due to the conglomeration of several key figures, namely the Outfit, who controlled bootlegging across the Great Lakes and throughout the interconnected rail networks."

"And there was money everywhere," Madeline explained. "Pouring out of the car and into the pond. I thought it was some sign from Heaven, but then Grandpa got at it, and it must've tainted it all because that's when hell broke loose."

A cacophony of sound mainly coming from B.J. and Brandy: "So the bull comes after me, I'm dressed like a clown, just not thinking straight at all -."

"Did you even know we have Mennonites in the redwood areas? I didn't. I think they're staging a ground war with the

Mormons. Seeing the Mennonites as well armed as they were."

"It could be seen as the first true large-scale example of late-stage capitalism creating a problem in order to sell a solution. This persisted beyond the initial prohibition period when methamphetamine production became --"

"Everybody, shush!" Jimmy insisted. All their words blended together in a confusing soup of details. He pointed to the boys first. "So you two stole a mob drop box, and now they want whatever was inside of it back. Right?"

"Right!" they both said. "See, I told you he would understand." The boys in unison.

Jimmy massaged his temples and tried to reel his anger in before it escaped like a twenty-pound bass and sank their boat.

"I understand I raised two morons!"

"All we have to do is find the thumb drive," Brandy said.

"Yeah, Dad," Hammer said. "They said they would leave if we gave it to them."

"They said they'd pay out a grand for it," B.J. added. "Awful nice of them to bother, y'know, paying us off as their hostages and whatnot."

"They did seem like nice gentlemen," Madeline said. They all turned and looked at her in total disbelief. Jimmy leaned forward in his chair and heard the thumping of doggy feet descending the stairs. He saw Wag with a plastic baggie in his mouth, seemingly stuck in his teeth, with a little swinging nub of a device in it. He spotted Wag before Wag realized he was even there.

"The thumb drive wouldn't happen to be a plastic bag, would it?" Jimmy asked. He eyed the dog calmly. Cotton came halfway down but sensed what was about to happen and ran up the stairs. Wag turned to follow until he heard the pump of the shotgun. Wag stopped in his tracks and turned around. Jimmy wasn't one to trifle with. For one, unlike Grandpa, he could *aim*.

Wag came downstairs slowly and dropped the baggie off at Jimmy's feet. He reached down and picked it up and put his pup on the head for him to go. Everyone was impressed. He couldn't wrangle his family at all, but he could heel a dog without a second thought.

"Now," he said, "let's go see what is so important about this drive."

The family went up to Brandy's room, a hip teen hangout room with everything scaled down a little bit for a nine-year-old girl. She had periodicals and encyclopedias, along with used textbooks and marked-up science journals on bookshelves all around her room. And a little play mat with some dollies marked in Sharpie as 'childhood therapy corner.' Most importantly, she had her desk and laptop.

She inserted the thumb drive - she was the only one who got

USBs right the first time, every time - and checked the contents. A piece of media tried to auto-play, so she let it run to see what the mob boss would see if he did the same. It was an overhead security camera video of an alley. Bruiser was there. He managed a stack of cash over to someone across the trunk lid dressed as a police officer of high rank.

"There's more coming," Bruiser said, "if you keep your troops out of our district. Got it? There's lots of money to be made for everyone.".

"Don't get stupid with my *troops,* and you won't have a problem." The officer sifted his hands through the money and did a quick count of the stacks. "Hey, you're a little light here. I've got expenses."

Bruiser reached into his jacket. There was a brief, tense stand-off before he pulled out another stack. Then another. He continued to unload as the officer scooped it all into a satchel, which he stowed into the back seat. During the brief pause, Bruiser turned his face up to the camera with a big, bright smile. The officer came back around and glanced up in the camera's direction but missed it.

"Something funny?" the officer asked.

"Just excited to be moving forward," Bruiser said.

"Yeah, yeah…"

The video went on like that. The preview showed the officer loading more money while Bruiser stood by and minded the camera.

B.J. had an idea. "Go to Google and request the name and image of the current Detroit Police Chief."

Brandy did so, took a screenshot from the video, unblurred and enhanced it with her Photoshop and got a decent half-profile shot of the officer. He looked nearly identical to the most updated picture of the police chief of Detroit. The only difference was he wore a hat during the deal. Same man, otherwise.

"Oh, land sake," Madeline sighed. "These are *not* nice people."

"Damn it," Jimmy said, "we didn't need this right now. Okay, so let's get the bad news out of the way. I harvested the major portion of the back 80 and sent it off to the co-op. We don't have enough to make the note." He got up and left the room.

"Are those betting numbers?" B.J. asked in a hush.

"It's the farm," Hammer said. "We got this bombshell piece of police corruption and modern-day kingpins, and he's thinking about the overhead right now."

B.J. nodded. "So what do we do with this?"

"This gets us our freedom," Brandy said, "but for what?"

"I'm going to check on your father," Madeline said. "You all email the President and see if you can't get him over the landline."

The younger set was left not knowing quite what to do, but it was clear that they had a higher priority than dealing with the mobsters at hand. Grandpa was missing, and worst of all, their dad was going off the debtor's deep end...

Chapter 14

Jimmy sat at the kitchen table and did the unthinkable: he sorted his bills. Every overdue draft notice and curtly worded bank letter was open in front of him. The envelope tablecloth turned into a cascade that flowed over the sides of the dining table. There was all the paper his family could eat, which was good, because it was the only fiber they might be able to afford at all soon.

Madeline, B.J. Hammer and Brandy eventually joined him for part two of their emergency family meeting. The immediate threat was dealt with, but the looming doom higher up in the sky still had no hope of stopping. Jimmy threw down a handful of papers on the table with a slap.

"We're losing the farm," Jimmy lamented. "We are three years behind on our note. Keeping up with modern farming techniques is very expensive, you know."

"There has to be something we can do," B.J. said.

"Not unless I can suddenly come up with another crop for the market this year, which I can't."

"What if," Hammer asked, "we knew a way for you to keep the farm and pay everything due?" B.J. looked to him like, really, do we? And he shrugged.

"There's not enough money in corn and wheat. I figure we

have less than a month before the bank and that damn corporate farm comes sniffing around here."

"There might be a way," B.J. said. "Brandy, we need a calculator."

She nodded and ran to the next room over and brought back an accountant's calculator with a fresh spool of wound-up paper tape.

"All right," she said, cracking her knuckles to begin, "37 bushels per acre times 80 square acres at $15.50. It comes out to $250.00 Per bushel times 37, which equals $9,250.00 per acre. Take out roughly 29.50 Per acre in cost, and you are still short, especially without the subsidies, Dad."

Everyone nodded, impressed, except for Jimmy. Her intellect and quick math only proved his doom was real.

"What if," B.J. asked, "we could plant that same acreage and harvest it three more times in a year?"

"We owe $300,000.00 in back mortgage right now," Jimmy said, shaking his head.

"It would only cut the note to $150,000.00," Brandy confirmed. "We need a crop that has a faster turnaround and greater return."

"Like what?" Jimmy asked.

The twins thought for a second. B.J. got nervous and pulled out his vape pen, which long since lost its charge and its juice, which gave them both the same idea, which they spoke together.

"Pot! Dad, it's one to two million dollars per acre!"

Jimmy looked at them like they just insulted their own mother to diss him. "I am not going to become a drug dealer to save this farm, selling pot to poor young kids who fry their brains. I have morals…." He looked up in thought and rolled the numbers around real quick. "15-20 million? Are you sure?" The boys looked excited, but the idea was brushed clean from the welcome mat of his brain. "Never mind."

"Why not, Dad?" Hammer asked. "I did it, and look how I turned out."

Jimmy looked at him. Then he turned to the other brother. "Anything to say, B.J.? Crickets! I am afraid he said it all. Convincingly, no less. Yes!"

"Cannabis is going to be legal in California very shortly," Brandy mentioned. "Prop 64 is on the ballot."

Jimmy tapped his finger against his mouth thoughtfully. Anything else to get out of the idea, or at the very least, any other holes in the idea that had to smooth out before he fell into it. "We don't have time to grow a whole new crop."

"B.J. and I," Hammer mentioned, "have been working on a growth hormone. It might work."

Jimmy looked at his children. One brilliant mathematician and two...he strained to ever call them scientists, but that's what they were. "Biological research and agricultural development at the University of San Jose. Both are summa cum laude."

"How long?"

"A week, more or less," B.J. said. He opened up a drawer and picked out a packet of tomato seeds, then went out the back through the kitchen door.

"Where are you going?" Madeline called out. B.J. worked out in the dark for a moment, then came back with a planter's pot of soil. He plopped the seeds in and covered them with some un-mulched, sun-baked dirt from around the house's trim.

"If this works, you two have to at least listen to us," he said. He reached into his pocket and produced a small, thin vial of liquid. Almost identical to his vape pen. He spread the moisture around in the dirt while the family watched with some bemusement.

"Does the term Horse Pucky, When Pigs Fly, oh wait, When Hell Freezes over mean anything to you?" Jimmy asked. "I have been a farmer my whole life. Nothing will make any crop grow that fast. Nothing." He sighed and rubbed his receding hairline with his hand. "All of you can sit there and watch Jack grow his beanstalk, but I'm tired." He turned away and started on a path upstairs. The kids motioned for Mom to get the thumb drive before he did.

Madeline swooped in behind him. "Oh honey," she said seductively, "I'll be right up. You'll feel better, I promise."

"Not a chance, Maddy," he grumbled.

Then, there was a slow onset of quietude in the home. Enough quiet that the sound of B.J. tapping his fingers on the counter could be heard. Something was not possible while a certain someone was around.

"Where's Grandpa?" Brandy whispered.

Just then, the door opened. B.J. scrambled for the nearest knife to defend himself.

It was Grandpa. The three stared him down.

"You're going to get us all killed, Grandpa," Hammer said.

"Kiss my tuchus," Grandpa snapped. "I was this close to getting laid, then those two city boys had to spoil it for me. I am going to watch some porn." He looked up past the ceiling with an accusing finger. "The deal is off."

With that, the whole family Monticeto was under the same roof, ripe plucking for their hounded hunters, with blackmail in hand and hope planted in the dirt....

Chapter 15

Sunshine broke through the musty, dusty windows of the Monticeto farmhouse. They traced a line of warmth across the wooden floor. Cotton lay splayed out to catch the rays over the sink. Wag paced around in the upstairs hallway while Jimmy lazily plodded his tired feet downstairs for another day of dread and misery. It was Sunday, so he could at least hold off on any real terrible thoughts until after church, but first, he had to make it there, which felt impossible as the weight of his debt dragged him down.

He saw B.J. and Hammer were already up, still on their broken eastern seaboard timelines. Eating tomatoes, whole and juicy ones. From a pot that they had between them on the table, which still had a few more fist-size reds to pick from. And they were smug about it, too. They expected some surprise. When Madeline came down, Jimmy nearly picked her up off the floor - nearly - and kissed her with joy. He stared at the massive plant with awe.

"Holy marinara sauce," he said. "Is that for real?

"Now, are you gonna listen?" B.J. asked.

"If this works, Dad," Hammer said, "one crop and you are free from the bank and that damn corporation. Think about it."

Jimmy sat down with the plant. It joined him for his morning cup of coffee.

"Maybe they're right," Madeline said as she served his drink. "We have lost touch with the way things are. You know that. By golly, when's the last time we were on a vacation or went somewhere exotic? We could do all that with that kind of money."

"Hey," he said, "I took you to Bakersfield just a few years ago, now that was exotic. We even got to see Buck Owens play. That's something you'll never forget."

"Who?"

"Oh my gosh! Buck Owens! Everyone knows who he is."

He turned to his sons, who were just waiting for the morning spat to end.

"We'll grow two test rows," Hammer offered. "I can't tell if the seeds are Indica or Sativa. It shouldn't take more than two days. Then we plant the entire crop."

Jimmy patted Hammer on the shoulder with approval. They would get to work immediately. However, first, they had to go to church. It would be a celebratory time. They'd be freed from their mob debt and, sooner rather than later, free of their land debt. Then they could make their own future, unbound by rules of law or land tax and truly untethered like a tumbleweed in the wind.

The church was packed with parishioners. It was a small, old-world-style church built in the early 1900s and never really renovated. It was a hotbox of old wood and metal joints that brought together all the heat of the NoCal sun and none of the shade under pure reflective-white paint.

Everyone dressed their best, including B.J., who wore very sensible knee shorts to keep a breeze going and sock garters to show he was still striving for formality. Grandpa had an old suit on. The prospector was old. Gold rush old. A suit that might have seen the breaking of the first railway to the West Coast.

They filed in and took their seats. The front row was occupied by out-of-towners, it seemed, and Pastor Porter was chatting with them all the way up until the beginning of service. The hymnals were brutal under the heat. Voices cracked like old paint in the sun. Then, the sermon came. Grandpa leaned back and got his napping posture ready. Madeline kept him awake with sequential kicks to his shin.

"Even," Pastor Porter began, always enthusiastic about every line, "as the confused residents of our fair state debate the merits of proposition sixty-four, God is not confused. No, God is not confused!... Can I get an amen?"

"Amen!" the parishioners replied in unison, except B.J. He alternated hands and made shoulder-high shrugging gestures until Hammer caught him and poked him to stop.

"First Corinthians chapter six-verse nineteen through twenty says treat your body as a temple of the spirit within you, whom you have from God. You are not your own, do you hear me, Amen! Each of them has been bought with a terrible and glorious price, so glorify God in your body. Do not defile yourself with that Mary Jo Juana. It will confuse you and send you straight to hell. Can I get an Amen?"

The parishioners summoned a rousing Amen, except for the Monticetos. They kept their hands in their laps and bowed their heads in prayer - and shame. They eyed one another. Their well-considered plan felt like it was in a slight freefall going downhill.

"As the humanitarian that I am known to be, I will allow both sides of the debate to be presented, but we all know...the Lord will prevail. Be sober-minded, be watchful. Your adversary, the Devil, prowls around like a roaring lion, seeking someone to devour. And now, with no further introduction, the king of cannabis, the patriarch of the pot, the wizard of weed, Dweezil Dawgg himself! The podium is yours."

Hammer and B.J. clapped briefly. No one else did. The rest of the congregation was silent as the D-A-W-Double-G, OG, the Real G, West Side Low Ride, and Kush King himself took the stage.

"Thank you, Pastor Porter," Dweezil said. "Yo, been listening to the man busts yo chops, that's because he ain't getting none."

The organist leaned back from his seat. "Yo, my main man, he ain't Catholic."

"Oh, well, he looks like he ain't getting it, anyway...."

"He has three kids," a parishioner in the front row yelled.

"Play something my main vein."

Dweezil checked the organist, who immediately hit up the backing riff of Mary Jane and gave Dweezil a line to run and a beat to follow. He freestyled over the beat but not with it. He sermonized while the organ harmonized.

"Yo, all you know is we need a little downtime. Y'all wanna be as uptight as your main man over here. Of course not. Don't fear the fersnizzle. We all need a little sizzle in life. You see what I am saying. Can I get an Amen?"

"Amen!" the parishioners called.

"Y'all never tried the magic dragon while making love to ya lady. Trust me, y'all will never go back. Remember, vote yes on Prop sixty- four! Can I get an Amen?"

"Amen!"

The Monticetos stood, and Amen as well, except for Grandpa. He finally snapped out of his nap in time for a bit of a late one with his hands up and waving. "Ameeen…"

"Peace, ya'll. Love from east to west."

It was the best church service ever. As if sent down from above, from the hallowed record label halls in the Olympian mounds of LA, a messenger delivered the gospel. Thou shalt grow, and it shall be danketh. Thus speaketh the Word.

Chapter 16

Farming is tough work. It takes a sturdy body, a steady mind and a lot of really boring work. But the payoff is always worth it. The thrill of growing something from scratch, feeding the Earth and producing its bounty is unmatched in any other field of work.

The Monticeto farm was abuzz with a reinvigorated work ethic. Hammer and B.J. were digging up rows of corn using hoes and shovels, supervised by Jimmy and followed by Brandy, who sewed the seeds in each newly rooted hole.

Cannabis seeds, of course. The sticky icky in an itty-bitty form. Normally, detritus in the roll of a blunt meant to be smoked, but sustained the right way, it produced healthy buds and leaves for a toke and squeeze. Unlike hidden farms in the middle of the woods or hydroponic labs in basements and garages, they had dozens of acres to go over, and a special trick to make it all work better.

Once the seeds were planted, Jimmy filled in the holes one by one. Once a row was done, B.J. and Hammer alternated turns, taking their special compound into the back of a weed sprayer and running it down the line.

It was good, honest work to produce a good, honest crop. With their chemical, combined with the already potent properties of the crop it was growing as they spoke, there would probably be some side effects to bear in mind.

"We should test the first batch out," B.J. said. "Just in case."

"Just in case we get bored," Hammer added.

"No, no, he's in the right," Jimmy said. "If you won't eat your crops, no one will. Unless you're intending to sell it as feed for pigs, they'll eat anything."

The boys went and unloaded their tools in the barn. The hole in the back was still there, no way to get new doors on it, so they shuttered it with the folding plastic tables left over from the reunion. They went out the front, then immediately doubled back around the side when they saw who was at the front.

"Dad," B.J. said, "we have company. And I don't think they're here from Publisher's Clearinghouse."

"Who are these people?" Hammer asked.

Jimmy went into the back of the house and looked through the window. They came in a white sedan, pale riders of death. Mr. Mortimer and Mr. Cantu are flanked by two toughs with built-up beach bodies.

"Didn't take long," he said.

Mr. Mortimer knocked on the door as one of the thugs flanked around the side to catch any stragglers. Jimmy gathered up his best bullshitting face and smiled wide. He tried to get everyone to stay calm and play along and opened the door.

"Mr. Mortimer!" he said. "What brings you out on this fine day?"

"I think you know what, Jimmy," the man said.

"Oh, come on in!" he said. He and Mr. Cantu walked in and took the best-looking seats they could find in the living room. The tough who hung with them mad-dogged Hammer, who kept a steady, cautious glare fixed on him with his arms crossed, swollen and hard from the long morning's work. Jimmy sat down on the sofa across from the affluent men.

"My associate," Mr. Mortimer waved, "Mr. Cantu from the Abyss Corporation."

Jimmy nodded. "Answer's same as it was the last hundred times. We aren't selling."

Mr. Cantu nodded. His smile was cryptic, pre-packaged, like he was wearing a lie. "That's a shame," was all he said, but it felt like a threat.

"For you," Jimmy nodded.

"You'll get fair market value," Mr. Cantu said, "and clean up your credit in the process. It's a win-win for everyone. If you wait, we'll pick up the property after you're evicted. No one wants that…." He sounded like he wanted that. "Think about your beautiful family."

THUD....

The thug turned in a start. He started to lurch at Hammer. Hammer shared his alertness and stood his ground. The men grappled briefly while the rest of the room turned to the sound of the hearty splatter.

A tomato from the test vine dropped. It was the size of a baseball - old school, regulation, a three-pounder that could send a man to the bench for a season with a solid connection. It over ripened and spilled open, with enough juice and sauce for a full bowl of salsa. Mr. Cantu stood up and approached the plant as a new bud sprouted out of the empty vine socket immediately. It was the rebirthing of a brand new baby-green tomato before his eyes. It expanded like a balloon in slow motion.

"Have you ever seen anything like that?" Mr. Cantu said.

"Never," Mr. Mortimer agreed. "What are you thinking?"

"We will own everything on this property very shortly, including that." Mr. Cantu's hand drifted greedily to touch the sacred vine. Jimmy zipped in front of him and moved the plant back.

"I don't think so."

The tough shrugged Hammer off and stepped alongside his bosses. "Who's gonna stop us?"

"You know something?" Hammer said. He scraped the tomato off the floor, the sacrificed fruit of his and his brother's labors, and let the juice flow into his hand like blood. "I really don't like you." He smooshed the remains of the tomato into the man's face.

"Hammer!" Madeline shouted.

The thug looked Hammer over, a smug and winning smile on his sweaty face. He lunged for the plant, picked a fresh one-off, and returned the favor. Hammer took it bravely - he was stunned. It was not the fight he was expecting, but not at all one he planned to lose. Meanwhile, the other goon circled fully around to the back near where B.J. held back inside the kitchen nook.

All while Mr. Middleton's crew watched from a distance away on the other side of the barn.

"This place is a zoo," Mr. Middleton said. "Get in there and help them."

Bruiser pointed at himself. Mr. Middleton firmly nodded. He sighed and got out of the car. He checked his pistol for ammo before he checked the car into park, so it slid back down the slope for a second while Mr. Middleton scrambled inside to get to the driver's seat.

The second thug, a bulldog-looking guy with flappy cheeks,

couldn't work the doorknob in time as B.J. locked it in his face, so he busted out and tried to crawl through the window. He got his leg up to lift himself through the door when he saw nothing but red.

"Get off the stage!" Grandpa shouted. He chucked a tomato full force and sent the other thug tumbling backward. The man got up, drew a gun, and drop-kicked the door in. B.J. fell with a shriek to the floor, and the thug was on top of him in no time. His gun was drawn and aimed down at the man on the floor. Hammer turned in shock and took a blind hook to his face that staggered him.

"I'm going to shove this gun up your -."

Click.

The thug couldn't finish his insult. That wasn't his gun that clicked. His gun didn't click, and it was semi-automatic. It came from behind. He raised his hand and let the gun dangle on his finger. Then he curled one hand and turned to retaliate. Bruiser floored him in one punch, right in the jaw as he spun. The bulldog man fell right next to B.J. like a refrigerator full of meat.

"Amateur," Bruiser said, shaking his hand loose. "And Gramps, don't you dare throw anymore -." He got hit with a tomato.

"Castle Doctrine, ya'll," Grandpa said with a chuckle.

The tables turned. Hammer turned his fist on his attacker and clocked him hard. Madeline slid over the counter into the kitchen and picked the first thing she could out of the nearest drawer to toss to B.J. - a frying pan. B.J. shot up and whacked Mr. Cantu in the head. It made the businessman reel and squelch his face with pain. He got a bruise, maybe some broken skin. Didn't really go down. Jimmy got clocked by Mr. Mortimer.

The thug in white grabbed the plant and tried to run out with it, but the vine was too tall to fit and hit the upper rim of the door. Mortimer tried to run, but Jimmy pounced his legs and wrestled him to the ground. They got entangled and fought their way out onto the front lawn.

"Get out the pots n' pans," Grandpa cheered. "We're having a scrap for dinner tonight!" He ran out for the front yard as Bruiser stepped back in. He grabbed a towel from the fridge handle, wiped it off, and threw it on the floor.

"Could you put that in the sink, please?" Madeline asked. He looked down at her, picked the cloth up and placed it in the sink. "Thank you."

"Don't mention it."

He and B.J. went out to continue the fight in the dust out front....

Chapter 17

The slugfest scuffle continued out on the front lawn. A veritable party bowl worth of dust was kicked up as B.J. and Bruiser continued their tussle. Vinny was still stuck in the doorway until Mr. Mortimer tackled him to get the plant through the doorway. Before he could stand up, Jimmy tackled him into the dust. His black suit turned instantly rusty-sand red, as did Jimmy's chest and pit-stained sweat marks on his shirt.

"Yeah," Jimmy said. "Who's your daddy now? Come on."

"Fine with me," Mr. Mortimer said. "Prepare to get your butt kicked."

The two men, one old and one fancy, assume classic Queensbury boxing stances while B.J. scoop-and-slammed the much heavier man in the background. It was like a diorama of fighting through history, with the oldest and most misguided attempts at the front while real action was obscured by fog in the back.

The difference was in skill. Despite looking pathetically old school, Mr. Mortimer had serious moves. He could dip, dodge and dive while Jimmy just stood there with his arms up and occasionally stretched them forward like he was a rockem sockem robot. He took a few blows while Mr. Middleton danced around him.

Milton stepped out but stayed on the porch to keep his tux from getting dirty. Mr. Middleton kept an agreeable distance and tried to nurse his head wound. The hazy exterior looked even more blurry, thanks to his growing concussion. But he wasn't free from fighting. Mr. Cantu darted out the door and threw a punch at the first man he saw, trapping the two old suits into a fight while Milton shrieked over it and backed away.

Milton saw Vinny annihilating Hammer in the distance and grabbed a broom to try and separate them, or help somehow. He ran over, broom held like a jousting stick, and got thrown back by just the suggestion of a punch coming his way. He rolled on the ground, suit stained red, which flipped a switch in his diva's heart. He ran up screaming and jumped onto Vinny's back, where he grappled hard and bit his ear. B.J. joined in from his tussle and bit Vinny on the leg.

"AAHHHHH!!"

"Hold him," Hammer said. He wound up a long, deep punch and threw it. Vinny twisted around, and the blow landed on Milton instead. Vinny's back was covered with dead weight, which rocked him forward, right into B.J.'s baseball swing of a cast iron skillet. The metal cracked. The skull, too. He went down, with Milton still on his back and buried under a man's muscle. B.J. nodded approvingly at his erstwhile enemy and turned to see how his Dad was doing.

Jimmy was on the ground with Mr. Mortimer over him,

raining punches down on his guard. He would up what looked like a finishing blow onto Jimmy's bruised face but was interrupted with a stiff blow to the back of the head from the grip of a pistol. Mr. Mortimer reeled forward and gasped in pain. Mr. Middleton stood over him with the gun in hand and looked it over.

"That usually knocks people out," he mumbled.

Mr. Mortimer rolled off of Jimmy and looked up at the source of his pain. The fighting came to an end. There was a gun now, and the fun was over. B.J. tried to hide behind the pan to protect his face, uncertain if it would really work.

"Let us go," Mr. Mortimer demanded, "or we'll call the cops."

Mr. Middleton sighed and took out a cell phone. He tossed it over, and it landed at Mr. Mortimer's feet.

"Go ahead," he nodded. Everyone looked at him like he was crazy, which really meant he was the only sane one there. Mr. Mortimer, understanding the situation, didn't make a move. "Yes, that's what I thought." He motioned to Jimmy. "Who are they?"

"That's," Jimmy pointed out, "Mr. Mortimer from the bank, and he's Mr. Cantu from the corporate farm up the road."

Grandpa stomped up to the porch with a shotgun breached open and unloaded. "I say we blast em' and bury them in the backyard!" Madeline came out with a cold Yoo-Hoo in her hand and waved it in the air. Grandpa grabbed it, dropped his gun and went back inside.

Jimmy managed to sit up enough to talk. "They have been trying to take the farm away from this family for as long as I can remember. Now they've got their chance. I didn't make the note."

Mr. Middleton nodded and looked the scene over. "How long do you have?"

Mr. Mortimer got up on his still-wobbling Bambi legs. "Thirty days," he declared, "and it will be my pleasure to throw your fat ass off here personally."

Mr. Middleton raised up his gun to remind everybody that he was the only one allowed to lose his temper. He waved it over toward the house and stood to the side. One by one, the members of the former scrap filtered into the house and sat around the table. Those that could. Vinny was down for the count and left out on the porch to be picked up as his handlers left.

Grandpa finished his Yoo-Hoo in time to notice that the fight was over, and he was too drunk on chocolate to do anything about it. B.J. and Milton were chatting in the corner, dusting each other off away from the unfolding drama while the rest of the businessmen waited for Jimmy to return from his retreat upstairs.

He finally came back down with a thumb drive, the source of at least one of their collective headaches. He handed it over to Mr. Middleton, who holstered his gun and nodded. He signaled to Bruiser, who got up and, reluctantly, threw Jimmy a wad of cash.

"Take care of your family," Mr. Middleton said. "They are...colorful, to say the least." He turned and noticed Milton and B.J. exchanging numbers in an overly flirtatious way.

"Milton," his father called. Milton turned with innocent eyes, then went back to batting them in B.J.'s direction.

"Ding-a-ling child if you get a mind to," B.J. said.

"Oh, geez," Bruiser moaned. "Get me outta here."

And so they did. They up and left. The Monticeto family was rid of one of their problems. The other sat at their dining table, bruised and busted up, no less aggrieved than when they arrived, and over an issue that wasn't nearly as easy to solve as gang politics...

Chapter 18

It was a dark and not-so-stormy night at the Abyss Chemical Company Laboratory. No rain or thunder. That didn't happen in the desert. What they did have was mid-80s heat near midnight and minimal air conditioning in the penny-pinching headquarters of the bio-research company.

They came out of the scuffle at the farm yard with an important find and needed to define all of the relative information that could make them into multi-billionaires.

Nobel Prize Chemist Dr. Emmett Beeker, an aged and scholarly man with huge ears and a tiny nose, bent over a microscope to analyze the chemical spectrum analysis of the extractions from the ever-growing tomato plant from the Monticeto farm. His assistant, Dr. Dexter Medfield, was also there, off to the side. Waiting for a breakthrough to be discovered so he could announce it first and take the credit.

"Hmm," Dr. Beeker mused as he peered through the microscope. "Nothing unusual, nitrogen, phosphorus, potassium. Plenty of micronutrients." He ruffled his prominent, wing-like mustache. "Ready another slide, please, Dr. Medfield."

Dr. Medfield nodded. He used a small pipette to place the liquid from the juiced plant into a slide and handed it over to Dr. Beeker.

"Dr. Beeker," Medfield said, "Mr. Cantu will be here in the morning. He expects a working magic formula."

Dr. Beeker looked up from the microscope, and his incredibly thick glasses came down over his eyes. "In the last five years, our state-of-the-art computers could not come up with this magic formula. Now we have twenty-four hours."

"Really, Doctor, that is not fair. The Abyss Corporation will cut off our funding if we don't come through with this formula. No money. Nothing!"

"That's just it!" Dr. Beeker exclaimed. His glasses hopped off his nose for a second, then snapped back down on his forehead. "We have found nothing! Nothing! Nothing! These samples are just normal, everyday, common garden variety plant food extracts! What is the secret sauce ingredient!?" He eyed the pipette with the sample still inside. He picked it up, looked it over and shakily aimed it into his mouth.

"No, Doctor! NO!" Medfield shouted. But he couldn't stop the squirt. Dr. Beeker gulped just as Medfield reached him in desperate reach. The jolt caused Beeker to drop the dropper to the floor. They both braced for the change that would occur, the horrible effects that were to follow - for science. And nothing happened.

Medfield sighed with relief. Dr. Beeker tried, but suddenly felt like choking himself. He was so happy he wanted to celebrate early with a colleague still in the room. Or he started choking from the serum inside his throat. Dr. Medfield assumed it was the latter.

"I'm calling 911!"

"No!" Beeker said, choking, his voice strained and twisted in pitch. "I insist, no!" He choked a little more until his voice sounded like a duck. "I need to sit down." Medfield raced over and got a stool for his colleague to sit down. He needed the slightly older old man alive so he could slap his own name on the established research.

He stood over Dr. Beeker as he recovered and went back to normal breathing again. Dr. Medfield patted him on the shoulder, then leaned down a bit hard as his eyes tracked to something else. He was locked onto the top of Dr. Beeker's head.

"This is extraordinary!"

"What is it?" Beeker asked.

Medfield observed as the pale old doctor's bald head started to replenish. Not just replenish, regrow. Strands of rich, brown hair sprouted from formerly dead roots, and the smooth head of the elder doctor grew thick and thrush with a full brush of slick brown hair. Dr. Beeker saw it soon enough as his fringe cascaded down past his own eyes. After just a minute, he went from bald and living with it to a geriatric hair metal rocker.

"How do you feel?" Medfield asked as he dared to touch the springy, live mane of hair.

Dr. Beeker leaned back. "I feel awesome!"

Medfield grabbed a small mirror and handed it over for Dr. Beeker to observe. "Look!"

Dr. Beeker took one look, and his eyes nearly bulged out of his head with shock. "Hand me those scissors," he demanded. Dr. Beeker clipped a sturdy sample out of his bangs and picked it up from his lap. He held it up and wiggled it around. "We have work to do." He started to chuckle deviously as Medfield prepared a hair-type slide. "My hair is not the only thing that has grown."

Dr. Beeker made a stiff march out of the room and up the laboratory stairs to exit into the parking lot. It was the middle of the night. A scant figure in a white coat out on the asphalt wasn't an odd sight on its own. His hair trailed behind him, and he kept brushing it out of his face on instinct. Which meant he couldn't see how it was changing, from tip to root, from a luscious deep brown to a glowing, radioactive green. He didn't notice it, but someone else did.

Mr. Cantu came back from the scuffle at the farmhouse, ready to throw some papers against the wall to vent his frustrations when he spotted a glow in the distance within his own company's parking lot. He pulled out some binoculars from his glovebox and watched the good doctor go on his way in a fluster to a small smart car.

Dr. Beeker opened his car and laid out across the front seat to get to his cell phone. He was in a rush and didn't need to waste time sitting down and setting himself up all properly as if he was about to drive off.

"We have to meet," he said as soon as the line picked up. "I have something that is going to change everything. I'll text you the skinny - oh my." He finally spotted the glow coming from his head as it hit and lit up every light-shaded interior of his car. He looked at himself in the rearview and screamed. His scream subsided into hysterical laughter, which was heard all the way in Mr. Cantu's car across the way. Ground was being broken, that was certain.

Chapter 19

After the whole row at the farmhouse, Mr. Middleton took his son and his loyal thug back into town. Hepzibah was dusty and lonely, like a quiet part of a city that evaded most efforts of reconstruction. Modern, but vacant. There were cars on the road, but they all drove like they were lost, theirs included.

They knew the hotel and a few of the locations that served edible food, but that was it. It was a far cry from where they came from and where they were aiming to end up. They had the thumb drive and their money. Nothing left to do but leave.

Bruiser drove along as chauffeur with Milton up front and the boss in the back. Bruiser couldn't shake a rising discontent, like a dread, that made him shrug as he turned each corner.

"Why didn't we just whack them?"

Mr. Middleton sighed, somewhat disappointed. "Because back there, we were more than just a carload of wise guys for once. Soon, we'll be back to the same old life, same old neighborhood and the same old us." He leaned back in his seat and closed his eyes. Milton seemed to disagree, but couldn't bring himself to voice it.

Bruiser turned the AC on high to mask his voice as he whispered across to Milton.

"What's up with you two?"

Milton looked at Bruiser with the same unspoken misgiving he failed to hold for his father. A bit of a fear. "Would you really have killed that family?"

Bruiser shrugged. "If the boss had said so."

Milton gasped in dramatic shock. "You know he has never killed anyone. Nobody!"

Bruiser looked confused. "But all those stories?"

"Helped him move up, and no one ever questioned them," Milton explained. "Mom made him promise to get out before she died. Dad lied to her. That's hard to forget."

Mr. Middleton still heard them, even over the whoosh of the air conditioning, which was funneled to hit him straight in the face. He turned away to the window, and the glint of the light and the heat off the glass and some bitter memories all nearly forced a tear out of his face, but he wiped it away before he had to explain it.

The car came up to the Queers bar on the main street, near the hotel. They were almost done with all the misery of the mess of a town. Mr. Middleton thought back to the skyline of Detroit, the ambiance of police sirens and shootouts, the appeal of the public crowds who shuffled from place to place, wishing desperately they could be anywhere else. He tried to miss it because that was where he was going to be soon.

His eye caught sight of something else. The theater across from their hotel had its marquee up, and the audition sign was gone. He sat up in shock.

"Stop," he commanded. Bruiser pulled over in the street, to the displeasure of the car behind him. Mr. Middleton got out and straightened up his suit. He marched straight over to the theater and signaled Bruiser to circle the block to pick him up later.

The inside of the classic old single-stage auditorium was bustling with activity. A whirlwind of preparations and practice was underway on the stage. The director was a chubby but spritely man who could flutter and dance with the young gender-somethings who filled his stage.

He spotted Mr. Middleton and waved him down. Mr. Middleton waved back and watched the director run towards him with quick steps up the aisle. They shook hands, and the director led Mr. Middleton up toward the stage.

"Everyone!" the director called. "Everyone! I would like to introduce our lead for the play, Mr. Smith."

Everyone applauded for Mr. Middleton under his false, totally obscure and non-suspect stage name. He was a bit embarrassed and pulled the director off to the side to have a quiet talk.

"I can't," he said, feeling disappointment even in his own voice. "They want me back in Detroit." The director shook his head almost mournfully, but really, he only showed an ounce of the sorrow Mr. Middleton was feeling.

"I know who you are," he said. Mr. Middleton was shocked. "I was a casting director in Detroit back when you had a shot. I also know what you do."

Again, Mr. Middleton was shocked. He flashed back to years before when he was a young teen with a sleek dancer's body in a leotard and fancy feathered cap. He gave it his all in those dreamy years, prancing around for musicals and waxing the Shakespearean poetic opposite the veteran stage actors of the local uptown haunts.

Back when Detroit had a future, before he changed his own past. He was pulled into gang life and thrown into a hasty marriage, one which barely lasted long enough to produce an heir and a spare. Disappointment was the standard of his life. A life perfectly reflected by the modern rot of the former capital of manufacturing.

Can't even have good memories in Detroit.

"Then why did you?" Mr. Middleton asked.

The director wrapped his small hands around Mr. Middleton's thick palm. "Because you have talent…" he said with a shaky, tear-jerking voice. "You're not defined by what you do unless you let it define you." He sucked in some air and ended up yelling through a cracking voice. "And because everyone deserves a second chance. Everyone!"

Everyone heard his falsetto crescendo and turned. The director kind of danced away, holding his eyes with the back of his sleeve. Mr. Middleton looked out to the performers, all eyes on him. Then, to the audience, which was empty but would soon become full and abundant with onlookers.

All strangers who would come from far and wide to observe a familiar play cast with some known and unknown faces, yet the story would be the same. Not defined by who was in it, but what roles they chose - which they worked for and earned!

Mr. Middleton, high on his own self-importance and the overall drama of the well-acted scene, grabbed one of the Othello audition placards and ran out. He scanned the street for Bruiser, but the car was not on the road. It was across the street. After so long, Bruiser just gave up and parked at the hotel. Mr. Middleton put the placard down at the entrance. He looked across the street, up to the penthouse where his last day of rent was set to expire soon.

"Sorry, baby," he sighed. He didn't know, but Milton was watching, and could see from a distance how apologetic his father was. Bruiser didn't. He was busy packing, throwing all their brought-along goods into a steamer trunk to fit into the back of the car for the long-haul home.

Chapter 20

It was time for the Detroit mafia to return to their homeland of blown-up corner stores, bombed-out apartments and modern-day criminal enterprise on the shores of the Great Lakes.

They all met at the car, Mr. Middleton, after a brief drink and smoke outside of the lobby and got in to begin the long drive. Bruiser took them out of the city on a scenic route through the lower valley foothills and crag, which had a splendor all of its own in the setting sunlight.

The only sound heard was the constant tone of the engine as it hit a highway speed stride into the desert. Mr. Middleton and Milton both looked out at the scenery but occasionally turned to look at one another. They met eyes and saw just what one another was feeling.

"Pull over."

Bruiser looked into the rearview to see what the issue was. The issue was a gun, which Mr. Middleton held. He clicked the safety off and held his own driver up. Milton's eyes were as big as dinner plates. Bruiser pressed the brakes and stopped short enough for the luggage to clatter around in the back.

"What are you doing?" he asked.

"Get out," Mr. Middleton demanded. He led, and the other

two exited the car as well. Mr. Middleton motioned with his gun for Bruiser to open the trunk. Milton was hiding, crouched down at the rear of the car, where Bruiser came around.

"You said he's never killed anyone!" Bruiser whispered.

"He hasn't," Milton said. "That I know about."

Bruiser stood by as Mr. Middleton rounded to the back and holstered his gun.

"You're on your own from here, Bruiser," he declared. "Milton and I are staying." Milton was excited, overjoyed even. Bruiser was just confused.

"You're not gonna whack me?" he asked.

Milton started to retrieve the suitcase with his life's wardrobe in it. "You've been watching too many gangster movies. This is our chance to do something good for someone. We're going to help that family."

"Why?" Bruiser asked. "They're morons."

The mobster and his son looked at one another.

"You are going to go back," Mr. Middleton ordered, "and tell everyone you whacked both of us for stealing the money. You will probably be promoted and have your own crew. Do we have a deal?"

Bruiser saw the two cooperating, him between them, and the garbage bag full of cash in Milton's hand. He reminded them that he was armed, too, and pulled out his own pistol to aim at Milton. "Or I could just take the money."

Mr. Middleton reached into his inner suit jacket. Bruiser tensed up, waiting for the quick draw. He wouldn't let his own son get shot just to prove a point, would he? To get the drop? Forget gangster movies, and this was straight out of The Good, The Bad and the Lions' Fans. Mr. Middleton pulled out the thumb drive and thumb-flicked it over. Bruiser caught it and let his gun arm go slack.

"This is all they want," he said.

Bruiser looked it over. It was the same one they got from Jimmy and his clan of weirdos. A whole lot of trouble on such a little piece of plastic. He smirked and holstered his gun. "Don't ever let me catch either of you in Detroit ever again. Capeesh?"

The father and son smiled brighter than they had under their previous employ.

"Capeesh, my friend," Mr. Middleton said. "Good luck."

Bruiser hopped into the car, sans luggage but with the mob's precious secrets in his shirt pocket. "If it means anything," he said in parting, "I learned a lot from you. Thank you."

Mr. Middleton tipped an invisible hat as Bruiser shifted the rental car into gear with a screech and rumbled off into the dusty evening, leaving his former partners and bosses behind in the amber-orange dust.

"He could have at least given us a ride back to town?" Milton said. "My feet are killing me."

Mr. Middleton hiked his foot up onto the luggage case as a prop rock. "Even now, now, very now, an old black ram Is tupping your white ewe. Arise, arise! Awake the snorting citizens with the bell, Or else the devil will make a grandsire of you. Arise, I say!"

He remained in character until Milton started clapping.

"Mom would be so proud," he said.

Mr. Middleton gave a very short bow and looked up at the sky. "I hope she's watching. We're going to need her help." He took his gun out once more and tossed it into the ditch on the side of the road. Milton did the same. They left their matching guns behind to pursue a better life in the slow ides of Hepzibah, a life of love and peace for themselves and each other among fair and friendly fellows.

They walked only briefly, each thinking of what lay ahead of them until a certain itch took them over.

"I can't do it," Milton said as he dropped the case. "It's like a pacifier or something."

"Yeah, get mine too," his father said.

Milton ran back, got the guns, dusted them off, and hid them in his coat. They were ready for peace, but peace in America had caveats.

After a long hike, a metaphorical baptism by dust in the desert valley winds, they got back to the main street and made a beeline straight for the hotel to check back in. They were tired, sweaty, a little frazzled, but overall seemed happy. They had enough money to buy up a whole block, but they got used to Canterbury's rustic charm and its immediate proximity to the theater.

"I need a drink," Mr. Middleton said. "A big one."

Milton's eyes wandered over to the brightest neon lights in town at the corner where Queers was.

"Speaking of which," Milton said, "I need to call B.J.!"

"TMI, son. T. M. I."

The father and son split to begin their new lives, apart but still close together. While Milton headed over to the bar with phone in hand, Mr. Middleton headed over to the theater to right his course at last. He picked up the placard on his way past the entrance and put it next to a trash bin as he entered the practice-in-progress main stage.

The actors were running one of the scenes lacking their lead just to make sure they could fill in the blanks when the time came. Mr. Middleton walked down, a shadowy figure in the dark room, and sat at the front row. The director spotted him from the side alley of the stage and flew down to sit behind him.

"I'm done," Mr. Middleton said.

"I figured as much," the director said. "Is this what you really want?"

Mr. Middleton looked around at the theater. It was old, but shapely. A humble house for wholesome productions. The opposite of the steel girder roofs without accents or brutalism of the city. "Never been more sure in my life," he said, taking in a deep breath of the slightly musty air. "I'm finally home."

"Well then," the director clapped, "it's time to get to work." And was it? Opening night was just a short few days away. They'd need a miraculously cultured actor, with stunning charisma and a fully memorized script of the play to fill in the role of Othello in time. And luckily, he found his way to them, delayed by decades, and from across the country, the star landed where it was always meant to be.

And that wasn't even the gayest thing happening in town. Milton went to the bar of the club. The bartender saw him coming, prancing in, a perfect fit for the early evening crowd.

"Yoo-hoo," Milton called. "Has B.J. been in?"

She responded, first, with his order - a cold glass of Yoo-Hoo right in front of him. "Why? You a cop or something?"

He looked at the drink, baffled, and shook his head. "Wrong, honey. Just a fan."

She nodded. The drink was still between them, and she figured out it wasn't what he was thirsty for. "Sorry, force of habit." She took the drink away, which prompted some curiosity in Milton.

It was a boy's night, mostly Twinks, and yet, for some reason, there were more Yoo-Hoo glasses around than beer. It was part of drinks, a substitute for water, and there was even a tall glass pyramid built up in the corner sectioned off for "recycling." Just another oddity of the small-town culture that Milton decided he'd learn to love...

Chapter 21

It was late evening at the Monticeto farmhouse. Most of the family was asleep. Jimmy and Madeline were slumped in their shared bed, utterly tired and wiped out from the hectic day of tragedy and slapstick combat. Jimmy's face was still red and swollen like he headbanged his way through a crowd of bees. Brandy was asleep in her room with a newspaper over her face. The downtrend of the markets put her on a similar downtrend to sleep.

Grandpa was just waking up and getting ready to head out on the town. His sleep schedule was all messed up, and he needed a quick spike of spicy chocolate drink to get it right. The brothers, likewise, slumbered on, but B.J. forgot to unset his phone alarm, which woke up Hammer.

Out of the two of them, B.J. did much more of the fighting and was more tuckered out. He didn't even stir or mumble when his phone tried to chirp him awake, but Hammer couldn't stand it. He nabbed it off the dresser and slid to silence it, which was when he saw the messages.

Meet you tonight

And a reply,

Already at Queers sounds good, which came in just minutes ago.

Hammer nudged B.J. to wake up. He didn't want him to miss a date or whatever. But B.J. wasn't getting up. He was also bruised and scuffed up from the brawl and probably couldn't show up even if he wanted to. So Hammer hatched a bit of a plan. He took a spritz of B.J.'s cologne, put on one of his loose baby tees and a pair of freshly sun-dried hot pants, styled his hair a little differently and went in his place.

He drove out in the dark a little before Grandpa left and got to Queers in plenty of time. He didn't so much approve of his brother trying to date one of the men who held them hostage earlier that day. Just a few hours ago. In waking memory. But he didn't want B.J. to look like a stand-up artist, and it'd hurt his little heart. Hammer took a deep breath in. "I feel pretty, so pretty." He approached the window on the door with a song in his heart and checked himself out. "Now I see the attraction to this...oh God, I'm gay."

He couldn't appreciate the revelation for long. The door swung open and clipped him into the bushes along the side. The two hearty bears who left didn't even notice they'd hit something and walked off to their ride-on motorcycle.

"Thanks," Hammer moaned. "I needed that."

He recovered and headed inside. Milton was easy to spot. He had a very city fashion about him, a big coat with fur lining. Everyone else was in some kind of cowboy chic, somewhere between a Texas drag show and a rural pride parade. Even people from further west near LA came dressed for the farmyard lifestyle or their idea of what it should be. Jeans and flannel cut short-short at every crevice.

Hammer made the gayest march he possibly could, walking on the heels of his feet with his butt up. He brushed some grass out of his hair along the way to look more presentable. He got just behind Milton and tapped him on the shoulder. Milton turned and looked his date over. Hammer gave him a wave the way B.J. would - curled his pointer finger to his thumb and jacked off the air. Milton fell for it and invited him to sit.

The ruse worked perfectly. Hammer got into character enough that he was impeccable as his own brother. Which frightened him, but it worked in the effort of getting close to Milton. He still didn't trust the guy, or his family, or the outfit their family hailed from. There was never an "enough" with mobsters, but there was always a hard way out. But first, they had to toast. Milton ordered them drinks from the bar and held them up.

"To you and your family. May you keep your farm and continue to thrive. Amen."

They both threw the shots back. Hammer wasn't prepared for the throat punch of whiskey on the rocks and coughed a bit as if he inhaled the very smoke that was used to age the barrel. Milton sipped his down, not quite as fast, but it was obvious even the water where he came from was a harder stuff to stomach.

"Two days ago," Hammer said, "you threatened to shoot us. I don't get it."

Milton locked down and rocked the ice in his glass. "Can I be honest with you, lover?"

"Lover?" Hammer shrilled. He turned to the bartender. "Refill, please. Now!" She was preoccupied. Milton put his hand over Hammer's. It scared Hammer stiff. The bartender finally came over to see what was going on. It was just Hammer, pointing to his glass like it was the only thing that could save him from his desperate situation. "Now! Make that a double, please. Keep 'em coming."

Milton gripped the hand harder, more sincerely.

"My dad and I," he explained, "had a revelation. We left the mob for good."

Hammer suddenly cooled down a lot. That was good, if true. It was one thing less to worry about. "What does that have to do with us?"

"It just so happens we have some money and time to help you save your farm. If you want help?"

Hammer nodded at the proposal. He was about to smack

SCOTT KINDRED

open his lips to discuss it when he noticed the swagger of a certain centenarian enter the bar. It was Grandpa, and as old as he was, he could still see through which of his grandsons was which.

"Crap!" Hammer cursed. He grabbed Milton's hand right back and yanked him off his seat. "Time to dance."

"Dance?"

"Yeah, sure!" Hammer exclaimed. "Why not? I love to dance. Come on, don't be such a - a prude." Hammer almost couldn't believe what he was saying but knew it was safer to get away from Grandpa than it was to get closer to Milton. They got entangled in the midst of the dance floor, face to face, while the rest of the patrons continued to groove and gyrate amongst each other.

Hammer did like to dance, but he wasn't familiar with bar dancing. He drew Milton into a tango to keep Milton away while the club played rap, and everyone around him did some variation of twerking. In a sense, they were the only couple dancing in the whole bar. Then everyone noticed who came in, and all attention turned to Grandpa.

"Elbert!" the bar cheered as he settled up to a seat. He waved them all on and threw up his hands to the beat.

"Yoo-Hoo, Elbert?" the bartender asked.

"On the rocks," he said, with an elbow brought down onto

128

the bar top. He nuzzled on up while she prepared the extremely straight forward drink. "You know that offer to knock boots is still open."

She laughed. "I am doing my best to resist it, Elbert, but it is getting harder."

He gave her the finger guns and took his drink, an ice-chilled Yoo-Hoo, and looked out at the crowd for new faces. It was a boy's night, mostly, no one for him in particular. But he did happen to notice the chic styles of Milton, which stood out from the crowd. They locked eyes just briefly while Milton was between the steps Hammer threw him in and out of. Hammer brought him back in to get his eyes off the bar. Milton turned Hammer around to evade his Grandpa's eye, and Hammer brought him around again.

"Wonderful dance, the waltz," Milton remarked. "Time to waltz."

"Right back at you," Hammer agreed.

The two danced at one another, competitively, to one-up the other and steal the lead, all while avoiding the encroaching suspicion of a syrup-water slurping elder. They realized simultaneously what they were both dancing for and worked together to avoid Grandpa in various steps and sweeps through the crowded floor.

"What do you say?" Milton asked. "Will you accept our

help, yes or no?"

"Foxtrot," Hammer called out. They segued immediately into a steppy, mobile dance that sent them around a very thick couple to block sight from a now-searching Elbert. "You're not gonna kill us or try and take the farm?"

"Tango again," they got close together to get smaller and blend in deeper with the rest of the crowd. "I don't want the farm. I just want to help. Your Grandpa is on to us. Yes or No!"

Hammer started to panic. "Foxtrot! I gotta talk to Dad. We need at least fifty for the chemicals and then more of the secret ingredient."

"Done," Milton said. "Seal it with a kiss."

Hammer froze up. Grandpa was upon him. Milton moved in, eyes closed, a standing dip. His lips met the hard, smooth surface of the back of Hammer's hand as he blocked the advance.

"Gentleman's…agreement," Hammer said. He removed his hand just as they were close and let the surrounding dancers believe it was a real kiss. That made them close in like living curtains for privacy and amorous fascination, which put a sturdy wall between them and Grandpa.

"Deal. Break!"

Both were in agreement and departed. They high-stepped

toward the exit while Grandpa pursued, unaware of their arrangement - or of his grandson's involvement. He just saw the top of Milton's stylishly smooth head depart through the back.

"Hammer?" Grandpa called. "Hammer!"

They were outside before long, running in tandem.

"Why is he calling you Hammer?" Milton asked.

Hammer kept his face turned away. Any light bright enough, and he might catch on to the trick.

"Alzheimer's," he answered. "I'll call you tomorrow with an answer, promise."

They fled to their respective cars, Hammer in his and Milton in a new rental. Both tore off in different directions, with Grandpa at the curb, watching them go. He gave them a heavy glare and sipped clean his Yoo-Hoo glass.

"Wow," he remarked. "You never know." He threw back what was left, including the ice, chewed it up between his few remaining good teeth, and swaggered back toward the bar. "Back to the hunt. Ladies, here I come. Yoo-Hoo!"

Chapter 22

The next day, the Monticeto family got together over breakfast to discuss how they were going to save the family farm going forward. They already had the solution, the miracle growth formula. The problem was they didn't have the materials, and a real estate hoarding autocratic corporation owner stole their one-proving test case for their homebrew growth formula, which could save their property. It was a big problem and required a large pot of coffee to wake up over. Jimmy had himself a third cup while Hammer finished his first.

"It's gonna take," Hammer explained, "at least fifty thousand to bring the pH levels up to where they need to be and to build the greenhouses."

"That's assuming I am all in on this pot thing, which I haven't said I am. I don't have fifty thousand lying around. Do you know where we can find a money tree?"

"I can get the money."

"Where?"

Hammer sipped foam off the rim of his cup. "It's not so much where but whom, Dad."

"Spit it out then, who?"

Hammer nodded and waited for his dad to sip so he wouldn't

be interrupted.

"Mr. Middleton."

Jimmy spat right back into his cup, and splattered coffee on the tabletop. "Wo! Wo! Wo! I am not taking money from the mob."

"They are out of the Mob," Hammer claimed. "They left it. They just want to help."

Jimmy looked at him in disbelief. "You mean like the last time when they threatened to kill us? No, dammit. No."

"Dad -."

"No!"

Jimmy picked up his coffee and left the room, with Hammer stunned at the sudden finality of their conversation. Madeline entered the kitchen and realized there was something bothering Hammer. She didn't catch the beginning or tail end of their conversation as it was. All she saw was her son upset and some specks of coffee staining the steam-cleaned tabletop. She sat down with a rag and wiped while she talked.

"Anything on your mind that you want to unload?"

Hammer rocked his cheek into his palm and rolled his neck around.

"Why is Dad so stubborn? I got the money for the crop, but

he won't take it. He's going to lose this place unless he takes the help."

"Where's the help coming from?"

"Mr. Middleton and his son, Milton. They left the mob and wanted to give us the money for the supplies. Milton said all they wanted to do was help."

Madeline finished wiping and went over to the fridge. She brought back a tomato and an orange and set them down in the middle of the table.

"Listen up. I will only get my daily nutrition from a fruit, not a vegetable. Which one should I choose?"

Hammer rolled his eyes at the tired, tested metaphor. "Mom, I know, come on."

"Which one, son," she insisted. She saw him hesitating, not wanting to go through the routine that she'd done since he was a child. "Land sakes, pick one. Stop being such a ninny, pick."

"The orange, of course."

"There you go, son. Both are fruits, but because one doesn't meet your expectations of what a fruit should be, you reject it. Change your Dad's picture. He sees this as Mafia money, right?" She picked up the tomato and took a big bite out of it like a sloppy apple. "You're the one not giving him choices. Change the picture, then you'll change the outcome."

Hammer was stunned, left with just the orange, while his mother took the tomato. Her message was subtle but clued him in on what he had to do next. He picked up the orange and rolled it around in his fingers.

"Who knew mom was that smart," he mused.

"I heard that," she called from the hall.

"And had that good of hearing," he mumbled.

"I can still hear you," she shouted.

"Crap," he whispered.

Hammer was determined to get that better picture in view for his dad to see. Words weren't enough to convince him of the sudden heel-face turn the Middleton's underwent in just a day, so he had to bring back the truth. He got in his car and headed out to the Canterbury Inn to meet up with either or and get them to bring back a positive testimony.

No one was there. The two were living their best life out of the hotel, integrating into the community during their daytime romps. Milton's romps were, predictably, more literal.

His father, however, was a topic of some minor discussion as a strange out-of-towner with an elegant air of respect about him and all the money the inn needed from a rich customer to run forever. And he spent most of his time when not touring around in a car at the theater across the road.

Hammer intruded on the private but open practice in the midst of a pageant of ridiculous performers. He wasn't one for the art of stage play. It was a bit too fancy for him. Mr. Middleton seemed to enjoy it as he pranced and made sweeping movements up on stage.

Just walking was a whole affair he underwent to make it as intense and poetic as possible. The rest of the actors, God bless them, were trying. They tried in the way the loser kid at a high school talent show tried by singing through thousands of voice cracks in a costume his mother made him, not knowing just how toxically cringe he was. And there were a dozen of them.

After so much, Hammer just couldn't take it and went to cool his jets in the bathroom. He returned as the actors all went on break, and Mr. Middleton was freed up. He was older than any of his fellow cast but far more in shape as he wiped his face down with a towel. Mr. Middleton approached the rough-and-tumble farm boy first.

"To what fortune do I owe this impromptu visit, Mr. Monticeto?"

Hammer nodded. He didn't want to dance around the issue, and there was no competition. He'd lose. It was clear Milton only got a fraction of his old man's performance genes. He also didn't want to waste the so-claimed former mobster's time.

"That money," Hammer said. "Did you get it by killing someone?"

Mr. Middleton perked an eyebrow. He could see the stern, straight-shooting Hammer was doing and the context behind it all. "I have never killed anyone in my life, and I intend to keep it that way."

"My father is an idiot. He won't take the money. He's going to lose the farm."

"Your father," Mr. Middleton corrected, "is a principled man who deserves respect. Remember that when you speak to me."

Hammer was taken aback. He didn't expect to face defense for his dad outside his own home. Someone must have knocked too much sense into the mobster's back during the farmhouse fight. "He's always lived by his values and never compromised. Look what it got him?"

"Why should he change now?"

Hammer nodded. He felt beaten. He couldn't counter a stranger's respect with his own indignance. "My brother and I want to help him save the farm."

Mr. Middleton nodded. He took a blank page from a nearby practice script and scribbled on it. He folded it up tight and handed it over. "Take this to him, and do not open it." Hammer reached out to claim it like it was some fragile, precious thing.

Mr. Middleton seized him by the wrist, and, with just a bit of force, drove into Hammer's mind just how powerless he really was against such a man. "Second thing, don't ever call Jimmy an idiot in front of me again."

Hammer nodded in shock and left with the note. After the fear subsided, he felt suddenly hopeful. He wasn't sure just how much of a corner he had with the Middleton's support, but if he was that willing to support and back up Jimmy, then maybe they really did have a proper fighting chance. They just needed their ringer back. The knockout formula to make some knockout weed.

Chapter 23

Hammer had the note in his possession. He didn't know exactly what it was, and the curiosity compelled him to take a glance. But he refused. The thought of Mr. Middleton getting mad and proving himself a liar in the realm of killing men, starting with Hammer, was too scary.

He was put in his place thoroughly by the gentleman mobster. If it was all just an act, then the Othello production would be a sweeping success in his performance alone.

He kept the note in his pocket and drove home to deliver it. That was simple enough. He saw his dad in the kitchen and slapped the note right in front of him.

"Gotta go shower, Dad," Hammer said. "I'm exhausted."

"Hey, where's my car?" Jimmy asked.

Hammer slid the keys across the table and made sure to hit the note. He was gone, and Jimmy was left with the conspicuous paper. He just couldn't help himself but open it up and read it, permission or not. What he saw first shocked, then elated him.

"Maddy!" he called out. "I have a surprise for you!"

The next day, things came up red-lettered. B.J. and Hammer woke extra early to catch the sunrise for the first part of their wake-and-bake ritual. The fields were rich with a dry, thin-leafed cannabis crop. Where corn once grew, now stalky bushes of spicy-scented weed grew.

They took the first harvested plant of many into the barn and carefully stripped it out on the remains of the welcome-back celebration tables, all stitched and stapled together. It was careful work and done fast. They had their seeds and leaves, the stock and lock of a proper blunt in the making.

Or proper herbs for a spiced dish, which came into play in the second part of their test run. Madeline was in the kitchen reading over a Betty Crocker cookbook for brownies to see if there was any section on herbal additives.

"Oh my stars," she exclaimed, "I'll just have to wing it."

The boys came in with a plastic mixing bowl full of their ingredients. They could smell the rich scent of mixed ingredients out of a bag.

"Oh yeah!" Hammer exclaimed. "Extra chocolaty, Mom."

"Dibs on the bowl," B.J. said.

They supplied the weed, and she incorporated it as best she could into the mix. Martha Stewart is damned for not including herbs in her baking handbook. The leaves and seeds were beaten together.

The THC in the oil was released through the baking. After

an hour, they had a university dorm breakfast: pot brownies served hot from the oven, extra fluffy thanks to fresh farmhouse eggs.

Jimmy, Hammer, B.J., Brandy, Grandpa and a curious Mr. Middleton all awaited at the dining table. He was there to observe the plan in action and back up Jimmy on whatever decision he concluded.

"Honey," Jimmy said, "sure smells wonderful!"

"Yummy, Mom," Brandy said.

"Thanks, hon," Madeline said. "They're fresh out of the oven. She placed the large tray down, all rich, dark, cakey edibles for the taking - but not all made equally. She picked one up that was made separate on a little paper plate and handed it to Brandy.

"Here, honey, I made this one special for you." Brandy took hers while everyone else helped themselves to what was on the tray. Brandy honed in on what was happening around her.

"I suppose it's not so special then," she said as she observed her plain brownie.

"Hey, Boo-Boo," Hammer said. "You're the control element in this experiment."

"As usual," she said. She joined the others and ate her snack while the rest experimented.

An hour later, the effects kicked in, and the entire family plus guests were left…kind of the same. Brandy noticed it. Some mild lethargy set in, but nothing else.

Mr. Middleton was left in a ruminant state on the couch, pondering quietly to himself what to make of it based on his own history of drug exposure while the family just kind of lazed around thoughtlessly.

"Dad," Brandy said, "I've decided that I am going to love poverty."

"That's not funny, Brandy!" Jimmy asserted. She gave him an overly sarcastic look, and he realized, too late, what she was doing. "Oh, I see what you mean. I'm supposed to be laughing hysterically right now." He gave out a few mild, fake laughs and then sighed. "I'm not at all hungry, either."

"It does seem," Brandy said, "that the active ingredient, tetrahydrocannabinol, doesn't work."

Mr. Middleton leaned forward in agreement. "Where exactly did you get the cannabis seeds, gentlemen?"

B.J. and Hammer both rose from their relaxed positions and answered in tandem, with a wary eye on the comatose-looking old man on the floor. "Grandpa's army foot locker."

That woke Grandpa up with a start and a fury. "You used my vintage Japanese Hokkaido Seima Kaisha seeds!? You knuckleheads! Those seeds were given to me by Emperor Hirohito himself as part of the peace reception gift when I attended the surrender ceremonies on board the New Jersey!"

Mr. Middleton, while dubious over Grandpa's grandiose claim to a historic moment, puzzled over the apparent truth. "So it would seem the potency of said seeds has diminished over some seventy-plus years."

"The seeds," Grandpa clarified, "not me." The boys tilted their heads a little at him. It was clear the crop wasn't as psychedelic as they were hoping; the effects were minimal, but there was undoubtedly a slight calmness in the air.

The drug content was low, but the crop was crop, and farm work had to progress. The two able-bodied boys used hand and mechanical tools alike to clear and bail all 90 acres of the cannabis plant, their home-grown bell pepper equivalent of weed. Which left them with a concern as it filled the storage of their barn.

"We can't keep it here," Hammer said.

B.J. snapped his fingers. "I have an idea."

The idea required a piece of machinery and a buyer. Hammer got a flatbed truck arranged with plenty of tarps to cover their product, which, while still illegal to grow or use, was technically not on their approved list of farm sales for the season.

If anyone had to ask, it was misshapen, overripe hay that got attacked by an army of skunks. Meanwhile, B.J. found a buyer through the hushed network of California farmers and producers. It was just a short drive north, up about to the place where they were almost killed by displaced Mennonites.

Hammer backed the flatbed into the Mennonite farm compound, some parts modern but mostly rustic and old school, and they met up with the proprietor, who looked slightly different without a shotgun aimed their way. He walked over from a cottage to their cab door.

"What hath thou brought us?" he asked.

B.J. climbed over Hammer in the driver's seat and perched up over him to answer out the window. "We hast brought thou bails upon bails of cannabis." He produced an official invoice for the merchandise and handed it down to the farmer with a pen.

"Thou hath brought a quill and ink, of course?" he asked.

"A quill with self-contained ink," B.J. pointed out.

The farmer licked the tip of the pen and judged the ink by its taste. It seemed good, so he wrote with it. "You both seem not to be such heathens from this day forward."

"We thank you," Hammer said, "for the tax write-off."

The farmer signed his name and claimed the weed. The farm

hands at the yard retrieved the entire quantity off the truck bed in mere minutes and left their flatbed more than a ton lighter. They set off to return with good news by evening and left the farmer and his son in their sideview mirrors.

"Hallelujah," the son calmly rejoiced, "we are saved, Father? The Lord hath given to us this day Puff the Magic Dragon."

The elder farmer looked with scrutiny at his son. "What is Puff the Magic Dragon?"

"Nothing, Father. We can make rope and other products from this. The Lord hath provided. Who is this from?"

He checked the invoice sheet. "It says Monticeto Farms. Put the bounty in the barn, Son."

The son looked at the bails upon bails mounted up in the yard in need of transport.

That night, there was a shadow in the barn, lit intermittently by the rhythmic stoking of a tindered light at the end of a stick. A soft light at first, but then stiffer and brighter, and then clouded by a wisp of smoke. The silhouette turned to its lantern and snuck out through the back entrance of the barn to stomp out a half-dragged joint in anger.

"Vile Heathen," the farmer hissed, "hath deceived me again. Puff the Magic Dragon is not herein. I hath been suckered!" Mildly outraged, the farmer went back to his home with tons and tons of perfectly legal, viable and cloth-alternative-friendly hemp instead of the barn full of dank he hoped for.

But a sale was a sale, and weed, however weak, was weed.

Chapter 24

An Abyss Corporation company car, a Crown Victoria, parked in front of the Monticeto household, a familiar and brutal stomping ground from days gone by. It seemed like weeks had passed since the scuffle, which put the Monticeto family on all the wrong maps, including the map of Mr. Cantu and his unfair weather enterprise.

The company car let out two hulking bruisers, Vinny and Bulldog, who looked at the house with great contention. Vinny rubbed his head.

The doctor said he'd still be smelling dog food when there wasn't any for a while, and Bulldog had to drain his ears to get the dirt out of them. It was a house of bad memories, and they intended to make some new ones even worse for the tenants.

They approached the house, unaware of the other visitors rolling down the drive in a Lincoln Town Car, freshly rented and waxed with dust-proof shine to keep it black and beautiful, just like the passengers Mr. Middleton and Milton. Their visit was mostly formal, but seeing trouble in sight, they stayed back and waited for an opportunity to help if necessary.

Vinny and Bulldog made their way along the worn grass path along the backside of the farmhouse, unaware they were being observed from afar. They crept up just out of sight, which led the reformed, former, never-killed-before gangsters to draw guns just in case and follow into the cornfield for cover.

Vinny got up to the house first with Bulldog close in tow and sided himself up next to a window. He heard some strange sounds coming from the inside and took a daring peek just into the window. Grandpa sat, pants on, shirt off with hole-covered socks kicked up on a recliner.

His eyes were glazed over, matching the mindlessness of what he was watching on TV. He had a cup of coffee in his hand that was still steaming. He lifted it up to his mouth, tasted it, and spat it back out.

"Who made this crap!?" he exclaimed. He hoisted himself up and stomped over to the window. He opened it up to get a breeze going. Grandpa's head was just in reach of Vinny's vice-grip knuckles.

He raised his arm up to nab the old man and yank him out like a radish. He was so ready to do it. Grandpa took another sip with a sour expression and gave up on the whole cup. He tossed it out to the side, into the bushes.

Right into Vinny's face. Vinny clutched his face and screamed. Bulldog yanked him back and covered his mouth. Grandpa stuck his head out the window and inspected the surroundings. The bushes rustled, but nothing was in them.

He retreated back inside and left the window open. The two thugs struggled quietly in the brush. Bulldog wiped Vinny's face down with his sleeve so only first-degree burns would settle in. Vinny was nearly gnashing at the teeth like a dog would do while his partner stayed calm and tried to keep them undetected.

Vinny stood up and approached the window again. Grandpa ducked his head out to meet him. Then he slid his shotgun out and squared up his aim. Vinny dove. The buckshot missed him and shredded the bush apart, which was just barely hiding Bulldog, who got up and ran as well.

"I ain't dying for this!" Bulldog shouted. Vinny caught up, and they ran in tandem and slalomed a bit as they went down the hill back toward the cornfield. Grandpa cocked his shotgun and aimed for a long shot. He pulled and hit the fleeing skeet right in the rear.

Instead of a shatter to confirm, he heard a yelp before the two pigeons were lost in the maze. Not only that, the two stopped screaming after some heavy fist-to-face hits were heard in the field. Grandpa ducked back inside just as Jimmy ran down to see not who fired the shotgun - it was obvious - but why?

"What in tarnations are you shooting at?"

"Those corporate Scally Wags are back. They tried to break in."

Jimmy threw out his arms in confusion. Then, all was answered by a knock at the door. Jimmy went to answer it with Grandpa covering him from behind with both barrels aimed from under Jimmy's arm.

He opened the door to greet the Middletons, who held a smile even with the gunpowder threat pointed their way. Jimmy pushed Grandpa's gun to the side and reluctantly led them in.

Chapter 25

Jimmy arranged a sit-down meeting with the Middletons. Grandpa was only allowed to participate if Madeline held his shotgun for him, which made him grumpy enough to refuse, so it was just the two fathers talking shop across the dining room table.

"I am just trying to help," Mr. Middleton said. "The money is not mafia money. It's personal. I have a few legitimate investments. I never planned on working for the mob forever. So..."

Jimmy remained skeptical but hopeful. He took the note out of his shirt pocket and held it up. "How do I know this offer is for real?"

"Because the interest rate and terms of the loan are from an FDIC-insured bank that I own. It is completely legit, Jimmy. I knew one day, my mob career would be over. Milton met B.J. Last night, and he told him the same thing."

Jimmy looked over to Milton, who nodded assuredly. "Your son met with Hammer, not B.J."

Mr. Middleton blinked to clear up his confusion. "No, he said it was B.J. I think my son knows the difference." Milton nodded proudly.

"I'm afraid you're wrong about that," Jimmy said respectfully. He then hollered up at the ceiling. "Hammer! Get down here! Now!" He returned to more personal tones to his guests. "B.J. slept all night."

Hammer came downstairs and saw what was going on. He spotted Milton and shrank back a bit, but it was okay. He was wearing different clothes, and days separated them, as well as lighting and the whole sense of self he gave off. Milton squinted to see if he knew, but he was too different.

But he smelled the same. Even after cycles of sweat and shower, B.J.'s long-lasting cologne clung to Hammer's body like stripper glitter. Milton looked shocked.

"B.J.!?"

"That is Hammer," Jimmy said. Hammer looked to his father in shock, like he'd been outed for some gross crime in front of an esteemed guest. "What's going on?"

B.J. also came downstairs after hearing the holler for Hammer, hoping his brother was getting in trouble, and he could watch. And that was the case, but once he learned what was happening - and why Milton was there looking him over extra hard, he got cross.

"You met him," B.J. said, "and pretended to be me?" Hammer couldn't look his brother in the face. "You -."

Milton leaned forward and punched Hammer in the mouth.

Mr. Middleton separated them immediately, although Hammer did not retaliate.

"Why?" B.J. asked.

"I was just trying to protect you," Hammer said. "Sorry." He looked to Milton as well, who was suffering from a bruised hand. "Sorry," he repeated.

"Enough!" Jimmy demanded. "Quiet, the both of you. Now!" The boys hung their heads in shame. Milton sulked in his seat and blew on his fingers to nurse his wound.

"May I interject some sanity?" Mr. Middleton offered.

"That would be an improvement," Jimmy nodded.

"Everyone sit," Mr. Middleton offered. He turned to Milton, who was still hot and bothered. "Please." He pointed to a chair for his son, and Milton reluctantly took it. Everyone else sat as well.

The ruckus summoned the rest of the family, who saw that things had already settled and it was safe to come in, unfortunately for Grandpa, who came down raring for another fight only to arrive while peace talks were underway.

Once everyone was assembled, Mr. Middleton made his case. "Hammer, I must commend you on covering for your brother. Milton gets a grip.

I just spent ten years of my life working for the MOB, and

you think we have a right to judge someone else? Really? Finally, B.J. and Jimmy, we really are legitimate businessmen who believe your farm can be saved, but you have to believe it first."

Grandpa pointed over to Jimmy. "There aren't a whole lot of lenders lining up to give you money in case you hadn't noticed."

"He's right," Madeline said. "Put your pride aside, honey."

Jimmy nodded and reflected. He considered his own attachments, his own reluctance and what it was based on. Trust was definitely an issue, but that was clearing up every moment the former mobster wasn't holding him up or asking for favors. Yet.

"What do you want?" Jimmy asked.

"The loan plus 15 percent and a lien on the mortgage till it is paid. That's it. No more than any other lender. It's fair, and you don't have to accept MOB money. It's legitimate." He reached into his pocket and unfolded some papers in front of Jimmy, spread out so he could review them each at his leisure. "I will have the money credited to your co-op account tomorrow."

Jimmy picked up the papers and read them over. Brandy came over to help and nodded along with what he was seeing. As far as loans and bank terms went, it all settled in his head.

Nothing too complicated, and no tiny subtexts that needed Grandpa's glasses to see. It was straightforward and totally fair, with a tidy profit margin for Mr. Middleton as well - a fair trade.

"Come on, Dad," B.J. said. "Sign it. Please."

Brandy looked up at her dad, having already finished reading it over. "The offer is already two percent under prime. What more do you want?"

Jimmy sighed. He felt worn down over an issue he never even had in the first place. Like he was being hassled to do something, he didn't even realize needed to be done the whole time.

"Fine, fine," he said. "I'll do it. Please, let this be real."

Mr. Middleton handed him a pen and pointed to two places on the paper to sign. Jimmy sat tight, sighed, and signed it away.

"Well," Mr. Middleton said, "that is everything we need to get started, right?" He turned to the head chemists for the farm's future botanical success.

"Well," B.J. said, "not exactly. The print on the label isn't correct. It's not Cherry Noble. It's Chornobyl, the nuclear power plant that had the meltdown. That's our secret ingredient. We have somebody on the inside to get us the seeds and the water from the reactor. For now, we have some water in our lab in New York.

We could have it here by tomorrow. The rest of it, the additional water and seeds, will take several days. We will just have to use what is available from the local area for now."

"I can get transportation out of Ukraine in two days. That's all the time I can give you. Can your contact meet them in time?"

"I think so. I'll get Victor on the phone right now."

B.J. got up and went upstairs, where he had the best reception, to dial up his old contacts via Victor. He put the call in. Almost halfway across the world, up in Ukraine near the border with Belarus, a phone rang in a hollowed-out Ukrainian warehouse.

What lay within was darkness, and in the darkness were guns held by a squadron of faceless troops molded into the shadows, aimed directly at two men: Victor and Leonard, two verified Stalkers of the zone. Victor, a haggard and world-weary man in his mid-20s, picked up the phone and chewed on the end of a long, wooden splinter more chopstick than a toothpick.

"Hey, Victor," B.J. said. "You got a minute?"

"I'm busy right now," he said in his Russian affectation. He put the phone on his shoulder and turned to Leonard. "It is the fruit bat." Leonard nodded sagely. Victor picked the phone back up. "What you want?"

"You all right?" B.J. asked.

"As you Americans say, how is it? Peach and keen?"

"I have a job for you, cash on the barrelhead, sweetness. I need some more sauce."

"Cash? Wonderful!" He looked up at the guns and those who held them. The barrels all lowered at once, a few inches, then raised back up when Victor smiled a bit too wide.

"When?" Leonard asked. He squeezed up to the call and masked his desperation with his deep, monotone voice.

"As soon as possible mister-phister. In 24 hours, for heaven's sake, hold on to your shorts. Have some patience."

"If I live long enough, I will," Leonard said.

"Doubtful," Victor mumbled.

"Unlikely," Leonard corrected. He swore at him in Russian and called him a simpleton. Victor hung up the call and dropped the cell phone, which was quickly raked away by someone's heavy military boot. The guns were raised and aimed at their heads still. Leonard looked up with a smile at the surrounding soldiers. He told them, in their native tongue, "You see, gentlemen, we will have your money very soon!"

B.J. was in luck, though he didn't know it. His sources weren't in a position to refuse even the most absurd last-minute request. He came downstairs triumphant, thinking he had made an expert negotiation, and faced the family gathering.

"Aaaand - We are ready to roll!" Milton clapped his hands and ran over to jump into B.J.'s arms. Hammer pumped his arm. Mr.

Middleton went across the table to Jimmy, who perched his forehead against his knuckles.

"Are you in?" Mr. Middleton asked.

Jimmy sighed one last short regret and nodded. "Let's do it."

They celebrated over shared bottles of beer, a brief victory sip before their efforts went into action and paid off.

Chapter 26

It came time for the Monticeto farms to start pushing its product. They got their first windfall of profits, a solid proof of concept, but needed branches that were more local to cut down on delivery costs and time. A quick turnaround meant quick profits, which meant quick repayment of the loan on their way to a fully functioning and officially saved family farm.

It was a hard business. It required marketing acumen, smooth dialogue with high-worth buyers and a social cleverness that Jimmy just didn't have. But he had a family to help him, and among them, the most social and wily spent his nights at a gay bar flirting and getting drunk on chocolate milk. So Brandy did it.

She called the City of Hope Hospital in the nearby city of Oatsdale, formerly Hope Springs, and got on the phone with the current head of the research department, Dr. Medfield.

"This is Dr. Medfield," he said, starting their negotiation.

"Hello, sir," Brandy began. Over the phone, she sounded like a high-voiced professional SoCal Valley agent. "I'm calling as a representative of Hephzibah's locally owned and organically grown free-range cannabis farm. I understand your hospital is undergoing research into alternative, natural anesthetics?"

"That's right."

"And, of course, cannabis has been considered within that research for its non-addictive pain-relieving effects?"

"Naturally," he said. "Not in a smoked form, but through extraction and concentration of THC, we can deliver a slow drip directly into patients, so they receive the maximal benefit that can't be achieved at home or in the back of a Winnebago."

Brandy laughed politely at the slight joke, then went straight into the dealing. "We can provide your hospital with at least twenty-one metric tons of cannabis this growing season."

"Impressive, but can you do it next year as well?"

"Next year, the yield goes up to 30 tons at market value."

Dr. Medfield was impressed. That number, with local rates sans import costs, would cut costs for the hospital and bulk their reserves up to the point where they could spend all their provisional funds and grant money on holidays for the whole staff.

With plenty of party favors to bring along. "All I need is the power of attorney so we can proceed. I think you should know how important this cannabis is going to be for thousands of sick patients with cancer glaucoma, and apparently, it's a cure for male pattern baldness. Who knew?!"

"Glad to help, Doctor. You'll have it in ten minutes along with our ...I mean, my client's bank information."

He checked his watch. From ten minutes out, the truck must have already been loaded up looking for a buyer. It was probably in town or close enough that it could make a cross-country drive without a hitch. He was impressed and slightly suspicious.

"I do have one question. What is your secret ingredient?"

"Ah, just like Coca-Cola, we can't give that away."

He nodded. "Here's some friendly advice: watch your backs."

They ended the discussion there. The sale was settled, but Brandy felt uneasy. His warning came at a somewhat inopportune moment. It took some of the wind from her sails. Her sales sails. The good ship weed farm was rocked around by the built-up suspicion of selling to the big hospital industry...

Chapter 27

Meanwhile, in Pripyat, Ukraine, Leonard and Victor sat in the back of an old Soviet-style tour bus. It still had a hammer and sickle painted onto the side, the only part of the moving mural of happy children and jacked soviet supermen that remained after years in the dank, swampy expanse of northern Ukraine.

The Stalker pair leaned back in their seats, loaded up with heavy gear that sealed them in tight from the radiation in the air. The rest of the tour bus was a mix of ages, none looking quite as prepared, from young children to elders who looked like they'd taken a blast of old Chornobyl right in the face at some point.

"Mr. Monticeto," Victor hushed, "says he pay us up front and residual in twenty days. We must make transport in Moscow by tomorrow. We get enough for two shipments to be safe. Da."

Leonard nodded. The Russian tour guide went on and on about the glorious soviet state's power efficiency and, the meddling of the West and secret wars undertaken since before the turn of the century - banal stuff they'd heard a thousand times before and didn't care to rehash. They were just in it for the fast entry to the exclusionary zone around the power plant.

The bus stopped to a stop just outside the town in view of the Ferris wheel. Passengers exited the bus with rebreather masks on and took pictures of the scenery. Victor and Leonard split from the group and made their way into the city proper.

They passed into a vacant building and took out their own gear. Victor held a Geiger counter, which was clicking away already, while Leonard got the water jug and testing kit.

"So simple," Victor said. "What I tell you. In, out." He snapped his gloved fingers.

"Precisely," Leonard agreed. "What could go -."

Victor smashed his mask against his face to cover his mouth. "Never say words!" he exclaimed.

"What words?" Leonard asked.

"What could go wrong," Victor said. He cursed at himself in Russian over saying it. He slapped Leonard on the back of the head.

"I am not simple, you simple!" Leonard protested. He waved the jug at him. Victor stared long and hard at him. His fury gave way, almost immediately, to fear. The hovel they took shelter in wasn't nearly as vacant as it looked. They were joined by a waking black bear. A bit of a big one. Normally about as big as a small man, living in the post-leak wilds made it a bit more bearish. It tilted its head at them and licked its jowls.

Victor and Leonard sauntered away and broke out in a run down the street. Meanwhile, the tour group was already packed up into the bus and ready to leave. The Russian tour guide noticed the empty seats in the back.

He didn't do anything about it. He just boarded, and they were off to the next stop. The two Stalkers were left in the dark to be stalked. The scenery of Pripyat was already creepy and unsettling. The evening just made it look far worse.

They proceeded through the old town the way they knew best into a rural area of overgrown plant life just in front of Chornobyl itself, under its great and massive steely coffin dome. They saw green fireflies and red ones, too. Or maybe those were eyes. Even the deer turned into predators in the untouched nuclear woods.

They arrived at their destination, an exposed stream with glistening water and glowing electric eels that swam around like streaks of neon lights in the dark. The eels hugged the banks of the water as the men walked into position. They heard something crunch a branch behind them and turned to inspect but saw nothing.

"Let's hurry," Leonard said.

"Da," Victor agreed. "I think somebody is watching us."

The dozens of creatures that surrounded them stalked them out of curiosity, and hungry interest remained at bay. They came to a small crossing, a narrow pass where the water was quick but shallow, just a few steps from one edge of the woods to the fields before the power plant.

Leonard looked down at the water. The living streak of light was gone. "Where did that green thing go? You know that thing could be green by itself. Not from ... you know."

"I bet that is true," Victor said. "You not prostok (simpleton) after all."

They both submerged themselves in the water and walked across. Their pants were sealed and waterproof, but they still felt the cold as the water rushed against them. Leonard looked down and saw the streaky green swimming between his legs. "See, boss," he said. "Is friendly."

He reached down to pet the eel. It reared its head up, and when it touched it, Leonard's skeleton lit up like a stack of fluorescent lights in the dark. Victor turned to see the strobing lights and the flashing faces of the myriad of creatures watching through the brush and trees with their dead, glowing eyes. He reached down to loosen Leonard's clutched grip on the eel and diffused the electricity between them.

"Let it go!" Victor strained through paralyzed teeth. "Let it go, you idiot!"

The eel finally slipped out of Leonard's hand like a long bar of soap and sent them both in a blast toward the shore. They landed in the rough grass and rolled around in pain for a moment. Victor's teeth clattered rapidly like he faced a blizzard. Leonard's hair was uncurled and stood out straight from the roots.

They straightened themselves out and proceeded unharmed through the rough field toward the power plant. They slipped past some caution tape and entered the grounds proper underneath the heinous concrete shell erected overhead.

It was like a cave the size of a city block, and inside was the root of all the world's problems with nuclear energy. They walked into the dark until they could follow some light, a soft green glow, down a long corridor. The Geiger counter was at a steady, mechanical growl as they approached the containment pool, which glowed with an emerald hue.

Leonard walked up to the edge and lowered his large glass jug down with some ropes. It slurped up the water and let out a few bubbles as it replaced the air with radioactive liquid. Victor took the other rope and pulled it up. They had about 55 gallons of enriched, radiant water. They set the jug down and waited for it to drip dry so they didn't have to touch it and risk further contamination. Victor turned on his phone. The radiation screwed with his signal, so he couldn't get any connection. He just needed some light.

A frog croaked nearby. Victor turned and put the flashlight

on it. It was not a normal frog. It had one bulbous growth in the middle of its head that rotated freely with a whole pupil inside. When it opened its mouth, Victor saw the light gleam of some sharp, pointy teeth.

"Hey Leonard," Victor said, "do frogs have teeth and growl at you?"

"That is the stupidest thing I ever heard," Leonard said. Then he saw it. "Oh, jumping, Jehoshaphat. That is ugly!"

The frog snarled at them and hissed. Suddenly, they heard a hundred more hissing amphibious beasts emerge out of the dark. The pool was suddenly alive, splashing from end to end. They grabbed their jug by the handles and ran for it, out of the reactor and into the field.

They were making a brisk pace when suddenly, the black bear reappeared and reared up on its hind legs with outstretched arms.

They ran along with the bear huffing behind them and jumped into the stream to cross it. And got electrocuted again. The animals of the woods scattered as the smoking men panted and screamed their way out like writhing demons from the morass of hell. The bear followed - also got shocked and was reduced to a pathetic limp.

Victor and Leonard were left shocked, beaten, bitten and bruised from their run through the city in the dead of night, but they preserved their precious water without spilling a drop. Their pay dirt, it was all worth it.

Even the faint glow they gave off was a worthy sacrifice for a free future. And they arrived just in time for the night tour to roll by. The same bus, same guide with different tourists. Victor and Leonard boarded without a word and sat in the back.

"I am finished," Victor said. "We send all the water to them. I will not come back here again. That's it. Da!"

"Da!" Leonard agreed. The tour guide came up to speak to them, maybe ask for their ticket or if they were okay. Victor waved him away with his gun to keep him quiet. They had contraband and didn't even care if they had to pay extra. The man was startled but not thoroughly scared until he saw the bear licking the window.

Everyone ran into the bus screaming. The vehicle peeled away with a screech on the old road and left the bear behind to waddle ineffectually after them.

Bindi the Circus Bear was left alone, once again, with no crowd to entertain. Poor Bindi. Someday, hopefully, a crowd will come who loves to see a dancing bear in the Pripyat wilderness...

Chapter 28

There was work to be done on the Monticeto farmstead. The first test batch was grown and sold. They needed the infrastructure, the setup, the groundwork and the labor to get the next load and the next, and the next, ready for harvest before their time came up. In order to save the family farm, the family had to use the letter F word, farm.

The men folk met a delivery truck up front, which pulled up and dropped off their new building materials: 1x4 boards and clear plastic rolls. These would turn into greenhouses that kept moisture in to keep the plants from drying out under the desert sun. It was the best way to get dank growth and was weather-resistant to keep water in but dry dust out.

And they could also hide the progress of their plantation. The vote, prop 64, was coming up soon. Even with marijuana legalization, industrial levels of harvest were restricted.

They couldn't wait for the papers to clear and the permissions to be passed along to the state authorities. They needed to get growing, and The Man could blow his own load about it.

Before construction began, Hammer and B.J. enlisted Brandy to help them collect soil samples from the field to test the pH and alkaline levels. They needed to set up greenhouses over the most ideal plots. The corn stalks could partially hide the structures, at least from ground level.

It would just look like simple tents across the field for separate growths of wetter crops. What crops? That was for the farming permit authorities to guess and for Mr. Middleton to insist they guessed wrong.

Once they got the right plots, the perfect stretches of land mixed in with the corn, they relocated some smaller spots of spoil together and got the tractor ready. Jimmy was their man. They loaded up a ton of seeds, stripped from their previous crop, and loaded up the auto-planter.

It was an old machine but a working one, greased up and ready to go. He made a long planting row, got off the tractor and checked his work. It'd been a while since he saw seeds sown into the dirt properly.

He walked over to the plot full of wacky weed seeds and touched his knees to the soil to pray.

"Dear Lord in heaven, by your grace did you grant this life unto our Earth and by our guile and power did we learn to craft it on our own. You made this plant, so I can't believe that you'd damn any one of us for growing it or using it in our…blessed sabbath from work.

Please, God, let this grow as it grew in the wild and grew alongside the honored American Indians for peace and prosperity. In your name, amen. I swear I'll be nicer to Elbert."

"Hey, Dad," Hammer said. Jimmy was startled and rolled onto his butt in the dirt when he saw his sons and daughter standing nearby. "You're not supposed to swear to God - that's what you told us."

"Still haven't gotten smitten yet," B.J. said. "And lord knows I've put some Lord in my."

"TMI, son," Jimmy refused.

"How do they look?" Hammer asked.

"Oh, it's a field, all right," Jimmy said as he pushed himself up. "Got them planted while it's dry, so the first big wet should shock them to life, and they'll get a-growin'. We gotta wait until morning if we want soft earth to work the poles in for the tents, but one night under the moon won't -."

Hammer and B.J. mounted up their spray kits.

"This is the last of what we had," Hammer said. "It's diluted, but ." "It's a little coffee with cream," B.J. said. "The straight cocaine injected through the eyeball mix should come in a few days."

"It better be worth it," Jimmy said. "I guess I'll keep

planting, and ya'll go ahead ."

The boys didn't wait for his approval. They lowered their masks and shot out a mist of slightly green chemical liquid that covered the ground. The soil moistened immediately like a sponge under a faucet, straight down to the seeds below.

While they prepared the first boost of nutrients, Madeline and Grandpa were preparing to set up the irrigation system. Rows of pipes needed tightening or loosening, and the sprinkler heads needed replacement as they'd all since rusted shut or been dinged up by passing tires.

Speaking of which, a Lincoln Town Car rolled into view. The co-signed loan owner of the farm, Mr. Middleton, arrived to check on the progress just in time to get enlisted to help.

They set up the irrigation system, hooked it up to the water main, and when the boys were done spraying, they prepared the first dousing from up the hill.

Gravity carried water from the pond down into the fields, and a mist of water came bursting up, which covered every acre in a veneer of water.

B.J. and Milton went for a run together in the fountains and slipped into the mud. B.J. tried to help him up, but neither of them really had a good grip, and both fell back down again. It became a train of slipping and falling and splashing in the mud for the rest of the family.

Hammer wadded up a ball of mud and gave it a quick underhand, which hit B.J. off his feet. Grandpa smothered Jimmy with a face full of mud, and Madeline slathered his head with so much mud that his body folded in half from the weight like a sandwich board.

Mr. Middleton took off his soaking-wet jacket and joined in the fun as well. The dark earth matched his skin to the point that most of the family couldn't tell if he was hit or not until his head was ballooned almost twice the size with packed on mud. But he laughed.

Everyone laughed.

They stank like compost, but they were happy.

Everyone took a break to wash off and went to work before evening getting the greenhouses erected. It was simple work with all of them together. Grandpa sat back with Wag and Cotton to watch and supervise. The crew stapled and nailed the plastic screens into assembled wooden square frames.

Then they joined the wood together in sturdy roofs and then up again on top of the walls. The greenhouses were risen one section at a time and got quicker as they went along.

The team stepped back and checked their progress. All the greenhouses were up, gathering moisture from the humidity, ensuring a warm and dank growth process for the plants underneath. Madeline prepared some lemonade for all. It was bitter and grassy.

"There was so much oil left over," she explained, "from brownie making, I decided to mix it into our lemonade."

"Mine tastes normal," Brandy pointed out.

"That's the way it should be, Boo-Boo," Hammer said.

"Any path unventured," Mr. Middleton mused. He swirled it around and tried to taste it again. It went from pleasantly sour to plain old bitter. "If you mixed this with vodka, you wouldn't be able to tell."

"Ooh, don't give me ideas," Milton said. He chugged it down.

The farm was ready but not quite finished. They still needed the secret ingredient, the super-powered growth formula, to kickstart the brunt of their blunt fields and make a miracle turnaround production.

Two days later, once the greenhouses were properly fogged up from the internal moisture buildup, their ingredients arrived. Fifty-five gallons from Cherry Noble Farms in otherwise unmarked liquid material.

The true contents were only known to the chemist brothers. It was well worth the price. It had to be. The shipment bill was enough to give Mr. Middleton heart palpitations.

B.J. and Hammer went straight to work to mix their chemicals. They got a good combination together and used a long wooden mallet to mush it all into a congealed form. This melted the mallet, which was a step in the right direction.

Just a little more base to counteract, and it would be golden. Once they were done, it shined with the most brilliant emerald glimmer, like the richest, iridescent matcha.

They connected nozzles to their tanker, filled an A.G. Chemical Mixing System and hooked it up to the tractor. They drove the portable canisters down to the field and worked the hose-led sprayers into each of the greenhouses to layer them with a coating of greenish water. The liquid sunk into the dark earth easily.

The long work was finally over. All that was left was to wait. The most desperate and dower time for farming, when everything was going well and time was the last obstacle, which meant that things could only possibly go worse.

Chapter 29

The Monticeto Farm took a long, well-deserved sleep following days upon days of work. As they slept, their plants would grow, and their money troubles would soon be over.

They would have crops, find sellers and harvest a profit, all under the watching eye of their then-made friend and loan tender. All was quiet in the field. The greenhouses were packed down and secured. Grandpa saw fit to place a lock on the vinyl flaps as an extra safety precaution.

But it wasn't enough. Not for the real threat to the crops. It wasn't muskrats or field mice or vultures. It was goons. Vinny and Bulldog, the Abyss Company thugs, returned after their health insurance-funded break to make a second attempt at the obstinate obstacles to their corporate agenda.

They came with two additions to their squad. Widow Maker, who was done up with a bunch of gnarly tattoos all over his face, and Will, an intern in his 30s. They carried red gas cans through the cornfield as quietly as possible, ready to tear down the whole place in the biggest, brightest way possible.

But they weren't quite enough. Not quite. Brandy was up late. She was reading some periodicals about modern farming and cannabis markets to grow her leads and market reach. But she heard something outside and got scared. She looked at her bed and her covers, which invited her to hide under them, but rationally decided against it. She was a big girl and did what a proper big girl should do: she went to get an adult.

She ran into Grandpa's room and shook him in his bed. "Grandpa, wake up," she said. "There's someone out there."

Grandpa rolled over in his onesie with the butt-hatch half unflipped and turned to her. "Awe, Myrna...I was just starting to Never mind. What?"

"There's someone in the field," Brandy said, pointing out the door.

Grandpa sighed and kicked his legs out from the bed. "Well, isn't that just grand?" He got up and walked into his coverall pants. "Go wake up your dad and stay here! Stay got it?"

She nodded and ran up to get her dad as well. Grandpa grabbed his keyring, which was stuffed completely with about fifty keys from current locks and locks from cars or houses he hadn't been to in decades.

He hopped and shuffled his way across the yard to the toolshed and tried the first key he could in the lock. Didn't work. He checked his keys and the old, dark iron lock on the door.

"All right," he said, looking up to the sky. "No more porn

for a month. Come on." He tested the next key. And it worked. He sighed with a pleasant smile. "I am a man of my word no more porn for a week." The cloudless sky rumbled with thunder.

"All right! All right," he said. He grabbed a nail gun off the wall and slotted in a battery like a magazine. "Time to play, punks." Grandpa stepped out and saw three figures stalking up out of the house. He aimed his nail gun at them and got a shotgun pointed his way.

"Oh, phew," Jimmy sighed. He had a shotgun loaded with rock salt pellets. "It's just you."

Hammer and B.J. kept their hands up. Just because it was Grandpa didn't mean they were safe. Fortunately, Grandpa was perfectly lucid and hyper-aware.

"Grab a shovel, each," he insisted. He hoisted his nail gun at Jimmy. "Trade you, fat ass."

Jimmy shook his head. "Keep dreaming, old man." Grandpa grimaced and followed Jimmy down to the field. The four thugs spread out to the corners of the field and sprayed spritzes of accelerant on the corners of each greenhouse as they walked around them. Grandpa stalked into the corn rows with his nail gun held up at his head tactically. B.J. and Hammer held their shovels over their shoulders like baseball bats.

"All right," Jimmy whispered. "Let's fan out."

"I smell gas," Hammer said.

"No, you don't," Grandpa said. "My anus is a steel trap at this time of night. It is my blessing and also my -."

"Different gas," B.J. said.

Grandpa took a whiff of the air and got stung by the sharp scent of hot methane. "They're gonna burn the crop!"

"Let's go," Jimmy insisted. He ran into the field.

"We're right behind you," Grandpa said. They filed in and then spread out.

"Let's get 'em before they strike a match," Jimmy said. The boys dispersed and tried to spring their trap on their respective targets. B.J. lay in wait as Widow Maker walked by. Once his back was turned, B.J. sprang up and smashed the shovel head into Widow Maker's skull, which did nothing. The grim goon turned with a smile elongated by the toothy grin tattoos that lined his cheeks.

"I am gonna kick your butt," Widow Maker growled.

"I believe you," B.J. said. He ran back into the corn. "Crap. Help!"

B.J.'s yelp signaled the rest of the goons that they weren't alone. Widow Maker stomped after B.J. about two steps, and

Hammer came up and layered on another stiff blow to the back of his head. Widow Maker stomped himself solid and turned with an empty-eyed, fearsome smile.

"Would you like fries with that, sir?" he asked. He turned a little more, went off balance and fell face down.

"What was that?" Hammer asked.

"The Terminator!" B.J. exclaimed as he stepped out from the cover. "Oh my God. My whole life just flashed before my eyes. It was disgusting."

The two ran back into the corn rows to stalk and spring themselves on the rest of the crew. Vinny was aware they were being hunted but wasn't ready to start the fire. For one, he was in the middle of the field. It's not the right place to start a fire.

Grandpa emerged from the corn with his gun up like he was a shadow stepping out of the dark. His body was smeared with a cover of dark mud, which helped him blend into the light night.

"Freeze, punk," he demanded. Vinny reached for his hip holster, but by the time he noticed, he was already completely held up. He froze. "I know what you're thinking. Did he shoot two-hundred nails or just one hundred and ninety-nine?

Well, at my age, I can't remember. But, being as how this is an eleven gauge Black and Decker, the most powerful nail gun in the world and would nail your head clean to the ground. You've got to ask yourself one question: "Do I feel lucky?" Well, do ya, punk?"

Vinny looked at his gun again and at Grandpa's gun. It was just a nail gun. He didn't think it was lethal. It's not as lethal as a regular gun. But the old man had hurt him badly before. Trauma dictated him to give up. He took it out of the holster with a pinch grip and tossed it over.

The standoff ended for both of them when a set of bright, white halogen lights kicked on and covered the field from afar. A bull horn squealed, and Deputy Delbert announced himself.

"All right, this is the Sheriff's department, Deputy Delbert here. We have you surrounded. Come out with your hands up." He squealed the bullhorn again. "That means you too, Grandpa."

"Surrounded!?" Grandpa protested. "There's only three of you knuckleheads. You couldn't surround anything except maybe a donut shop!"

"We heard that Grandpa! You're not really helping here."

"Wait a minute!" Vinny exclaimed. "I've got to know!"

Grandpa reaimed at Vinny and squeezed the trigger. Vinny got squeamish, winced, turned away, held his hands up and CLICK. Nothing.

"Get to stepping, punk," Grandpa warned. He reloaded the

181

nail gun from a pocket in his long johns.

"Grandpa," Hammer called out, "you okay?"

"Yeah," Grandpa said. Hammer emerged from the corn. "Watch him. I gotta go see where your dad is." Grandpa disappeared back into the corn and left Hammer to guard Vinny.

However, he also left Hammer unguarded and quiet, unassuming. Will crept up behind him. And behind him, in a procession of stealthy ambushes, was Jimmy. Jimmy waited for Will to get close to Hammer, enough to lower his guard, and he fired.

Red hot rock salt pellets smacked Will and Hammer on their rears. They both fell forward. Will was worse for wear, being just an intern who came in regular business slacks. A little hot pepper shot in the butt was not that bad for Hammer.

"Ow, dammit, that hurts!" he exclaimed.

Will started to get up first. Hammer jumped up, grabbed Vinny's gun and pointed the gun at him to hold him up. Will wasn't sure what to do. He jerked and jiggled in place, prepping which way to go to avoid him, but got smacked in the back of the head by B.J. and fell down to the ground. Jimmy walked forward with the threat properly neutralized.

"Sorry, son. I am really sorry. Are you okay?" Hammer nodded. Jimmy saw Vinny moving behind Hammer and aimed his shotgun right next to and past Hammer's head. "Both of you stay still." Vinny raised his hands and put them over his head.

"I'm fine," Hammer said. "Me and B.J. got one on the other side. Grandpa got this one." He pointed to Vinny. "That leaves just one. Grandpa is going after him now."

Bulldog swerved in and out from the rows of corn and got to a safe distance away, right at the edge of the gas they poured. He pulled out a simple gas station Bic lighter and held it up over his head. "Yo, one flick of my Bic should do the trick! Hey, I'm a poet, and I didn't even know it."

Grandpa stalked out of the corn and poked the nozzle of his nail gun right against Bulldog's buttcheck horizontally. He was poised to seal up at least one of the goon's holes for good. "Isn't that just swell! One pull and you're done, oh, and you aren't having any more fun. I hate poetry and punk. Drop It!"

Then Grandpa got held up by Delbert.

"Drop it, Grandpa. I got it from here."

"Don't be a killjoy, for Pete's sake, Delbert. It's sort of become a tradition to shoot him in the ass."

"Not it hasn't," Bulldog said. "Don't let him do it, Deputy." His voice quivered slightly. Delbert motioned for Grandpa to put the gun down. Grandpa rolled his eyes. Delbert insisted just under the sound of Bulldog quivering.

Grandpa lifted one of his hands off the gun, prepared to lower it, flipped Delbert the bird and let out a quick puff of the pressurized gun. The nail sank deep into the thug's butt, and he screamed. Grandpa shrugged and dropped the gun as Delbert held him up.

"Sorry," Grandpa said. "An accident."

"Old man," Bulldog whined, "I am gonna get you. He shot me again. That's twice."

"Well, I'll be," Grandpa said. "He can count. Wonders never cease."

"Where are the rest of them, Grandpa?" Delbert demanded.

"On the other side with Jimmy," Grandpa said. "I got this one. Let's Go."

Chapter 30

The farmhouse field at night was lit up with the police and, later, ambulance lights. Flashing strobes of blue and red covered the field and reflected off the white walls of the greenhouse tents. The four thugs were loaded into ambulances, along with Hammer, to treat his singed butt.

B.J., Jimmy and Grandpa were in custody with their arms behind their backs. Madeline and Brandy watched from nearby. Delbert came up to them once the situation was under control.

"They were just defending themselves," Madeline said. "Those bad guys came here and -." Delbert put his hands up to slow her down. "I'm glad you called Aunt Maddy before someone got hurt. We're not charging them with assault."

She was relieved. Delbert hiked up his pants to continue. "They're being charged with illegal cannabis possession and intent to distribute. We will have somebody come by from the DEA to clear the fields. I will help you guys any way I can, but this is way out of my league."

Madeline teared up and sobbed. "All these years. We're going to lose the farm, Delbert. All these years. Ain't this a real hoot?"

"I thought you were family," Brandy exclaimed. "Some

family you are!" She stormed off and slammed the door on the deputy. He sighed and shook his head a little.

"She's just frustrated," Madeline said. "She doesn't mean it."

"I know," he nodded. "Do you need anything?" Madeline shook her head. She just needed time.

Brandy, on the other hand, needed time alone. To get on her cell phone. She dialed someone up and waited for the line to connect. "Yes, this is his accountant. Oh, you received a sample.

We have forty more acres where that came from...Checking account number? Yes, I am authorized to sign for Mr. Monticeto." She headed up to her room to keep the business alive while the workforce and namesakes were taken away.

Madeline came inside and watched Delbert through the window as he organized around with the rest of his midnight skeleton crew. He looked inside his patrol car, where Jimmy and Grandpa took up the back seat. Grandpa was still slathered with mud and used that to bogart all the seats up to the middle and force Jimmy to squish against the door. B.J. was in the passenger seat on good-boy behavior. All the handcuffs were used on the near-arsonists so no one in the family was bound up.

"Let's go," Delbert said.

"Is Hammer going to be okay?" B.J. asked.

"He's fine," he said. "He'll be joining you after he's checked by the Doc."

Delbert and the Sheriff's crew pulled out, sandwiching the ambulances and drove out of the farmhouse drive, right past Mr. Cantu and Mr. Mortimer across the way.

They were waiting for their men to come back and saw, quite obviously, that wasn't going to happen. But they did see that the farmhouse was more or less emptied out of the usual old guard. It was just them and the tired, sad state of the wife and daughter left over.

The men walked over to the front door. Mr. Mortimer knocked, and Madeline, grumpily, answered.

"Did you come here to gloat?" she asked. "Because it's too late."

"Where's Jimmy?" Mr. Mortimer asked.

"You know exactly where he's at," she snapped. "Just leave."

Madeline moved to slam the door shut, but Mr. Cantu stuck his foot in the doorway. He sucked in air from the pain as the heavy door folded part of his leather shoe into his foot, and it sprung off. She grabbed the door to slam again, but Mr. Cantu pulled out his gun.

"In another 11 hours, 55 minutes and 40 seconds," he said, holding his watch up, "we will own this dump. Back up, In the living room. I like to be sure."

He pushed his way in and backed Madeline into the living room. She took a seat on the couch. She'd gotten used to the operations of being held as a hostage. It was annoying but no longer something novel or uncertain.

Mr. Mortimer closed the door and looked around to inspect the nearby halls, just in case. Brandy came down the stairs with a big smile on her face.

"Mom, I did it!" she exclaimed. She crested the stairs and saw what was going on. "Oh, boy."

"Sit," Mr. Cantu demanded. "I wasn't asking."

Brandy came down sheepishly and sat next to Madeline. Mr. Cantu took a seat across from them and kicked his feet up onto the coffee table with some pain at first. Then he settled down and kept his gun leveled on the arm rest at the girls.

"You know," Brandy said, "you're a real piece of shi -."

"Does your dad know you talk like that?" Mr. Mortimer chastised.

"My dad is going to kick your butt," Brandy said.

"The last time your dad tried, I gave him a knuckle sandwich, kid. Now, just sit there and shut up."

Brandy huffed and crossed her arms. Time ticked by, and the situation didn't improve. Brandy went from annoyed to aggrieved to twitching. She looked at the clock and started to shake a little. First, her head wobbled back and forth, and then her body started to shake and jerk around. She started to whine, which signaled Madeline to her daughter's issues.

"What's wrong with the kid?" Mr. Mortimer asked.

"Tourette's Syndrome," Madeline said. "We can't stress her out too much, or she does that."

Brandy started to convulse even worse and twitched out. The two men were creeped out. Her back arched, and she went into a reverse crab pose on the couch. "Mom," Brandy whined, "I want to watch Barney. I love you; you love me. We're one big happy family. Mom, I'm hungry."

"For tater tots and cereal," Madeline nodded knowingly. "Tater tots are the secret ingredient."

"Damn!" Mr. Cantu exclaimed. "Quit with the whining already! Give her a shot of vodka or something!"

"She needs rest, Lots of rest. It could get real ugly if she doesn't rest."

Brandy twitched harder and started singing in a droning vibrato. "I love you, you love me. We're one big happy family.

Hello, I'm Barney and you are?"

"Shut up!" Mr. Mortimer shouted. "It would be justifiable. Let's shoot them both."

"Doo-doo head," Brandy cursed. "You are a mean person."

"I've got both their phones," Mr. Cantu said. "Go to your room and watch TV. Don't try and leave, or we shoot your mom."

Brandy slumped off the couch and started to crawl across the floor toward the stairs. "Do-do head. Barney doesn't like you, and my dad is still going to kick your butt."

"Go!" Mr. Mortimer shouted. Brandy trudged up the stairs to her room, twitching the whole way. Once she was out of sight, she shook off her act and returned to normal.

She was free, phoneless, but not without any power. She was confident she was smarter than the armed thugs downstairs. In fact, she was out to prove it.

Chapter 31

Deputy Delbert and Sheriff Lloyd sat around their desks doing the extensive paperwork to file and settle all of the charges they needed to file against the Monticeto family and their home invaders. It was the slow and terrible side of being a police officer. Small town or not, every day either began or ended with too much paperwork.

Jimmy, Grandpa, B.J. and a butt-bandaged Hammer sat in the cell opposite Elmer, Hakeen and Esteban - their cell mates - who all looked around suspiciously. Grandpa stood up and started an impassioned, patriotic speech to his fellow jailbirds.

"All coppers are villains. If they get you in the restroom, out come the batons. Watch out for your privates."

Delbert approached the jail cell, out of earshot of the rant. "Would any of you like some coffee?"

"See?" Grandpa said. "Sly villains. Next, he'll be offering lattes and flavored creamer, mark my words."

"Uncle Elbert, come on," Delbert said. "All I have is milk."

"None for me, thank you," Jimmy said. "Deputy Sir. I am not talking to you. I know my rights. These guys are probably informants."

"Oh, that hurts, senior," Esteban said. "Maricon. Pinche'

191

Cabron. Just when I thought we could all just get along!"

Delbert shook his head and walked over to Sheriff Lloyd. The old, grizzled, gray-haired handlebar, mustached former gun toter had all the evidence laid out on a table.

The shovels were tagged, and the Black and Decker nail gun was in a thick blue bag, unloaded. Another bag was full of brownies taken from the kitchen, along with a shotgun. The bottle of diet Dr. Pepper was for the Sheriff.

"Well, they can't stay here," Lloyd said.

"What are we going to do?" Delbert asked.

"I am going on a hunger strike," Grandpa shouted. He then proceeded to loudly sing the Star-Spangled Banner. The other three cell mates joined in, leaving Jimmy and his sons out and cold-shouldered. Grandpa was officially on the other side of the cell, away from his family, uniting with his good-hearted strangers.

Sheriff Lloyd sighed. "Oh please, get Buck Owens and his gang over there out of here. I need to sort these guys out!"

The telephone rang. Deputy Mel picked it up, nodded to the receiver, and looked over at the sheriff. "Sheriff, it's Marcela. She wants to know what you want for dinner."

"Tell her spaghetti with those little hot dogs she puts in it. They're great. Oh, tell her not to worry about dessert. I'll bring that home." He took a big whiff out of the brownie bag and let it spin around in his head a little before he sighed it out. "Where were we? Oh yes. This." He poked his hand at the other bags. "Is this what they defended their home with, against guns, real guns!?"

"Yes, Sheriff," Delbert said.

"And those four knuckleheads from the Abyss Corporation are in the hospital right now?"

"Uh-huh. Two with bumps on their heads and the other two with ballistic traumas to the buttocks."

"I see."

"Me too. It wasn't pretty, let me tell you."

"Hey!" Grandpa shouted. "Yoo-Hoo!"

"What?" Lloyd shouted back.

"No, damn it! Do you have any Yoo-Hoo? I'm parched! Hunger strikes make me thirsty!"

Mel chimed in. "I have one left over from last night's...church social." She took one out of her lunch bag and walked it over to the cell.

"Thank you, darlin," he said with a wink. "Say, haven't I seen you somewhere before?"

"Uh, I don't think so," she said. Grandpa clutched the bottle greedily and savored its sight before he quenched his thirsty throat.

B.J. sat over with the other inmates, who moved away from him on instinct. "So, what are you in for?" he asked Elmer, the biggest and nastiest looking strong man in the cell.

"Tax evasion," he said. "And resisting arrest."

"I'll get you next time, Elmer!" Delbert yelled.

Elmer stomped up and hopped toward the cell, hyped up and roided with rage. "Oh yeah? Bring it on, Scooter!"

"By the way, thanks for mowing my Mom's lawn."

"Anytime," Elmer replied. He turned back to B.J. "She's a wonderful woman."

"Yeah, Aunt Donna is great," B.J. agreed.

"Kill anybody?" Hammer asked Hakeem.

"No," he shook his head and smiled. "But...the night's not over yet."

Hammer nodded affirmatively and turned away.

Jimmy looked at Esteban and shrugged to see if he would go along with the inquiry.

"Parking tickets. Muchos tiquetes de parqueo. It's always the Spanish guy that gets it first. Me acusaron falsamente."

"I second that," Jimmy said. "Whatever he said."

Sheriff Lloyd tried to hide behind his telephone from the ruckus in his cells, but the call ended, and it wasn't good. "Delbert, that was the Assistant D.A. He's not pressing charges in this case. So the Monticeto boys and Grandpa are free to go."

"But Sheriff, what about that other matter? The herbal refreshment?"

The Sheriff looked at the brownies and got a glint in his eye. "With all this excitement, you forgot to keep tabs on the local ballot measures. Prop sixty-four passed."

Jimmy, B.J. and Hammer all sighed together with a deep, profound relief together.

"Thank God," Jimmy sighed.

"I'll take them home," Delbert said, also thankful.

"Thanks," Lloyd said. "It's getting a little crowded in here."

"To what?" Jimmy asked. "We will lose the farm in 20 minutes. We didn't make the note. It's over." It was a slightly somber victory walk as the boys were let out of the cell. The only hold-up was Grandpa, who decided he liked his new friends better than his family until he was convinced to come home to his bed and his booze.

Chapter 32

Brandy was at her computer, something the bad guys downstairs didn't know she had or knew how to use. She opened up the family account on the Hephzibah state bank website. It was more hers than the family's since she was the one who set it up and routed it to the business and everything.

The password was even hers: "tater tots." She got out her checkbook - her mom's, but really, hers - and got into the bank account to check their progress. To see if Mr. Middleton's loan went through and that they had the money for the initial debt.

And they did. $29,475,231 and ten cents.

"Yes!" she yelped. She clicked through to make a payment, pressed enter and the new debt balance came back as zero.

Mr. Cantu, downstairs, checked on his phone for the time. There were mere minutes left until the debt was due, and the seizure and ownership transferral would be completed. But something got in the way.

He got a notice from his email with the subject line of payment made. The normally positive message sent a chill through his spine. He checked the message and confirmed it. He looked up at the stairs.

"She's in the account!" Cantu said with a shudder.

"How?" Mr. Mortimer asked. "She's just a kid!"

Madeline started to get up, but Mr. Mortimer pointed his gun at her. Mr. Cantu got up and ran for the stairs.

Brandy rolled two dusty bowling balls out of her closet and pushed them to the edge of the stairs. As soon as she saw someone enter the view of the stairwell, she nudged one over the top stair and let it roll, then bounce, down the stairs.

It got some air, nearly reached Mr. Cantu's face and fell down to impact him on his chest as he leaned away to avoid it. It sent him flying back, and he hit his back and head hard on the floor.

"Bill?" Mr. Mortimer said. "Bill, are you all right?" He ran over to check. He peeked around the corner to see Mr. Cantu laid out with a bowling ball pressed onto his chest. He heard a loud thudding coming down the stairs.

He turned to face it just as the next ball bounced down one step, three steps, and then nearly reached Mr. Mortimer. He stepped back to dodge it, and it bounced perfectly off the edge of the step, which angled it into a sharp bounce straight up into his family jewels.

He screeched with great pain and fell down on top of Mr. Cantu's lap with enough force to make the prone man sit up. The bowling ball in his chest lifted up like a hammer and slammed into

Mr. Mortimer's back.

Mr. Mortimer shot forward, then fell back and was left laying on top of Mr. Cantu with the bowling ball between them. Brandy pumped her arm triumphantly. Madeline finally got up and inspected what all the noise was about. She saw both her captors prone on the floor, crushed by the big, weighty balls of Brandy.

The early morning sun rose over the horizon east of Hephzibah. Over the wide-open plains, the dusty rolling desert, and the Monticeto farm in the distance.

Deputy Delbert was on the way with a host of defeated and unfortunate men awaiting their grim fate. And one sleeping, snoring Grandpa. Delbert's phone rang with an emergency siren sound. He flipped it open and held it up.

"Hey, that's illegal, mister," B.J. chided. Delbert ignored him and kept his face stiff and stern.

"All right, Aunt Maddy," he said. Jimmy leaned forward. "Just stay hidden. We are on our way." He snapped the phone shut and tossed it into the center console.

"What's going on?" Jimmy asked.

"Mr. Mortimer and that guy from the corporate farm down the way, are holding Aunt Maddy and Brandy hostage at the house." Delbert flicked on the siren lights and hauled ass to the farmstead.

They exited the car in formation. Delbert crept up with his gun drawn. Jimmy ran past him.

"Jimmy," he called out, "you can't help her if you're dead. Go around the other side of the house." Jimmy nodded and ran around to the side and checked the nearest window while Delbert checked from the front porch. Both of them looked into the living room and saw that they were much too late.

Brandy jumped off the bottom stair onto Mr. Cantu's crotch and dug her heel in. The old man screamed in pain and curled up. It seemed like the emergency was pretty much over.

But Mr. Mortimer was made of some harder stuff. His balls were harder than the bowling ones. He shot up and wrangled an arm around Brandy in an instant and armed himself with his free hand. He'd had enough. What was one dead body to get a little even? He readied himself to pull the trigger and BANG.

And he fell over, skull partially flattened by the baseball swing of a frying pan. He dropped the gun and Brandy on his way down. Madeline stood over him, assertive and daring. Mr. Mortimer recovered partially, just enough to baby-deer-leg his way across the room as his head swam in its own excess juices, only to run into a blockage shaped like two legs. Belonging to Jimmy, who looked ready to kick his butt.

Delbert walked in, handcuffed at the ready; he'd seen all he needed to see.

"NO!" Jimmy insisted. "He's mine."

Mortimer managed to push himself to his feet and started cackling. "Your first beating wasn't enough. Do yourself a favor and let your nephew, Daisy Duke, do his job before you get hurt." Delbert stepped in, peacekeeper that he was, and haymakers Mortimer right in his smug face.

He spun on his heel with ballerina-like grace until he came to a stop and looked them both in the face. "I didn't see that coming." Then he fell down, for real. Delbert cuffed them both and slapped the cuffs on extra hard on Mortimer's arms.

"No one calls me Daisy Duke," he huffed.

Mr. Middleton and Milton pulled up when they noticed the lights strobing from up the street and saw their adversaries wrapped up and in the midst of being taken away. Milton ducked away from the lights on instinct, learned from his hoodlum life as a mob prince.

The day was won, but Mortimer remained cocksure and arrogant all the way up to the police car doors. "You're too late!" he cackled. "We own everything! And soon we'll own the police station, and the bars, and the water supply, and the air that you wannabe rednecks breathe!"

"Nuh-uh!" Brandy taunted. "I made the payment in time.

Paid in full, Mr. Poo-poo head!" She stuck out her tongue.

Mortimer scoffed. "With what? Play money?"

"Twenty-nine million dollars is a great start," Brandy said. She turned to her father, who was pleasantly surprised. "We're rich, dad!" The Monticeto family ran together and hugged each other. Mr. Mortimer was shoved into the car and looked at his boss.

Mr. Cantu nodded in confirmation. They had nothing except a few trespassing, invasion, hostage and assault charges. And the deep well of legal funds from the Abyss corporation, so they would be fine eventually, maybe settle out-of-court.

The bad guys lost, and the good family won. And that was cause for much celebration...

Chapter 33

The next evening, Grandpa got on his best suit, cleaned and pressed and ready for mingling. He drove his John Deere through the town for about thirty minutes until he arrived at Queers for his evening romp. He nudged his leg in through the door and slid to a stop with his arms up and legs open wide.

"Elbert!" the crowd cheered.

"Time to party!" he called out. "I'm rich! Well, technically, fat ass is."

He swagger-walked his way to the bar like a pimp bobblehead and sat next to a thick woman in an all-blue uniform Mel, from the police station.

"So, you're the infamous Elbert from Infamous Farms," she remarked. "I should have known."

Grandpa snapped his fingers at the bones, too, at her. "One hundred percent certified and bona fide. Speaking of bones, what's your name? I've seen you before. The jail. You're a real firecracker."

"Easy, cowboy," she said. "Slow your roll there."

He wrinkled his nose and started to turn. Another swing and a miss from playing a different ball game. She detected his dejection and smile. "I didn't say I play for the other team, handsome. I just work here part-time for some extra scratch."

He turned to her just in time to catch her winking.

"In that case," he said, slicking his hands against his greased hair to wick his fuzzy eyebrows into shape, "let's kick up our boots on the dance floor and shake off this dust."

"I'll be off in a few minutes," she said, "and I would love to."

Grandpa let out a wheeze, like the first air out of a collapsed cave since it was sealed many decades ago. "Are you sure, really? Are you feeling okay?" He was nearly jumping for joy over it, and the rest of the bar followed suit to get hyped up. It was a gay old time at the gay old bar…

And while some enjoyed the bright lights and loud music, others chose to attend a softer-lit but more proudly spoken form of entertainment. Othello was on stage, and Othello himself, Mr. Middleton, guided the performance with true deftness.

"I took by the throat the circumcised dog And smote him, thus." He took up a knife and, very realistically, stabbed at himself. A blood squib went off under his shirt and leaked his white cloth deep red.

Lodovico gasped. "O bloody period!"

Gratiano exclaimed. "All that's spoken is marr'd."

Othello knelt. "I kiss'd thee ere I kill'd thee: no way but this; Killing myself, to die upon a kiss." He fell onto a bed and died.

Cassio grieved. "This did I fear, but thought he had no weapon; For he was great of heart."

And Lodovico turned then to Iago for the closing monologue. "O Spartan dog, more fell than anguish, hunger, or the sea! Look on the tragic loading of this bed; This is thy work: the object poisons sight; Let it be hidden.

Gratiano, keep the house and seize upon the fortunes of the Moor, For they succeed on you. To you, lord governor remains the censure of this hellish villain; the time, the place, the torture: O, enforce it! Myself will straight aboard: and to the state this heavy act with heavy heart relate..."

The stage went dark, and the house lights turned on, revealing a packed crowd. A standing ovation occurred. Everyone local, Sheriff Lloyd and his wife Marcela, the Monticeto family, Doctors Medfield and Beeker whose hair was reduced back to a slightly green stubble, the Abyss corporation thugs in handcuffs and striped clothes, Mr. Cantu with a house arrest bracelet and parole officer, Mr. Mortimer in a Hannibal mask; even Bruiser came all the way down from Detroit with Mr. Giovanni to take in the way-out culture of a certain desert hot spot.

Mr. Middleton led the cast in a proud, regal bow as the

curtains came down.

After the performance, the cast was greeted by friends, family and a few stray fans. Mr. Middleton had some lady callers, middle-aged women who seemed to fancy his fine acting and fatherly demeanor.

And he had an admirer, apparently, in Jimmy, who greeted him with a bundle of flowers with suspiciously deep green leaves wreathed around the heads, along with an envelope. Jimmy motioned for him to open it.

It contained a check for $100,000. Mr. Middleton was more than happy - he was proud. It was his night to shine and be praised, yet he had just the same praise and goodwill for his earnest new friend.

They all left together, out the door and almost across the street to the hotel. But there was traffic. A single, solitary tractor of traffic with an illegal second passenger who had her arms wrapped around Grandpa's waist. Delbert stepped out to stop him. Grandpa gave him the finger and drove away - not any faster, just more rudely. Delbert was about to step off the curb to give chase, but Madeline held him back.

They all went to the Canterbury Hotel, drinks all around, and party favors freshly picked, courtesy of the local cannabis farm, legalized under Prop 64.

And the whole of the serene scene of good surviving past the greedy clutches of evil was observed from on high, from the saintly vision hazed by a cloud of fine smoke of an angelic patron of the breathable arts.

"Yeah, boy," Dweezil said. "Check out the sizzle on the fersnizzle. Know what I'm saying, man?"

"Oh yeah," the Mennonite patriarch said, sighing out a thick white cloud. "Righteous. Puff the magic dragon is sizzling. This is good shit, man. This is sizzling my nizzle!"

Dweezil took a toke. "Thou speaketh the truth, my brother." The farmer handed over his joint, his eyes rolled up, and he passed out on the roof. Dweezil double-fisted the joints and laid a blanket of exhale over the happily ever after ending.

"Amen."

EPILOGUE

After long hours of blissful peace, where even Grandpa Elbert's house of cards stood the test of time, a shriek that could be measured on the Richter scale permeated the air. A 10 that brought the cards down to the table. "Oh my stars!" like the rebel yell, sent chills through all who heard it.

If that was not a motivation for the rat, whose paws and feet were soiling the Monticeto's living room carpet with a black crude, to skedaddle, chased by Cotton and her sidekick Wag out the front door, the caboose on this critter train is an angry Madeline with her broom, swinging for the center field seats is!

About the Author

Scott Kindred's Author Bio

Scott Kindred: Bringing Stories to Life, On and Off the Page

I'm Scott Kindred, a storyteller born and raised in the stunning landscapes of Portland, Oregon. My passion for crafting narratives began at a young age – I remember writing my first stories when I was just seven years old. From that moment, I knew that my calling was to share intriguing, humorous, and exhilarating tales with the world, and this passion has only grown stronger over the years.

Shaping the Storyteller

After my time at Benson Polytechnic High School, where I honed my skills as a wordsmith by years of writing for the school paper, I continued my educational journey at Portland State University. Later, I further expanded on my technical expertise at the renowned Divers Institute of Technology in Seattle, Washington.

The Birth of *Cannabis Farms: A New Crop*

Our debut book, *Cannabis Farms: A New Crop*, was born during my stint at Warner Brothers, thanks to a collaborative spark with my friend, Lloyd Shellenberger. Recognizing the story's potential, I dedicated myself to transforming the concept into a promising narrative.

This novel marks the beginning of a series that follows the Monticeto family and their farm from the end of the Civil War to the present day. Each novel will be comprised of the escapades and hijinks of the new generation as they discover their place in the world.

Beyond the Words

These days, I call Southern California home, both living and working amidst the vibrant creative landscape. When I'm not busy at my writing desk, you'll find me corresponding with Lloyd and collaborating with various studios in the entertainment industry, adding my creative touch to the fascinating world of entertainment.

Scott Kindred & Lloyd Shellenberger Joint About Us

Two Worlds, One Story: The Inspiring Collaboration of Scott Kindred and Lloyd Shellenberger

Meet the dynamic duo behind the groundbreaking story of *Cannabis Farms* – a captivating tale woven from the threads of two distinct worlds. Scott Kindred, a storyteller and luminary in the entertainment industry, crossed paths with Lloyd Shellenberger, a retired broadcast journalist with 43 years of military service and a yearning to entertain people with his words.

Their serendipitous meeting while working at Warner Bros. marked the inception of an extraordinary partnership. Lloyd approached Scott with the raw essence of a story, and Scott, with an innate knack for storytelling, breathed life into it.

Now, you too can revel in their collaborative masterpiece and Scott Kindred's debut novel – *Cannabis Farms: A New Crop* is available now!

Made in the USA
Las Vegas, NV
03 December 2023

82041118R00125